Anonymous

Rebel brag and British bluster:

A record of unfulfilled prophecies, baffled schemes, and disappointed hopes

Anonymous

Rebel brag and British bluster:
A record of unfulfilled prophecies, baffled schemes, and disappointed hopes

ISBN/EAN: 9783337730413

Printed in Europe, USA, Canada, Australia, Japan

Cover: Foto ©ninafisch / pixelio.de

More available books at **www.hansebooks.com**

AND

BRITISH BLUSTER;

A RECORD OF

UNFULFILLED PROPHECIES, BAFFLED SCHEMES, AND DIS-
APPOINTED HOPES, WITH ECHOES OF VERY IN-
SIGNIFICANT THUNDER. VERY PLEASANT
TO READ AND INSTRUCTIVE TO
ALL WHO ARE CAPABLE OF
LEARNING.

By OWLS-GLASS.

NEW YORK:
THE AMERICAN NEWS COMPANY.
119 & 121 Nassau, St.

PREFATORY NOTE.

It must not be thought that the following pages are the fruit of a search through the British journals for articles upon our late civil war. Life is too short for such an employment of time without prospect of much greater benefit, public and private, than that task could accomplish, however effectually performed. The articles, extracts from which are here reprinted were, with many others, cut out and laid aside in the course of the current perusal of British journals during the war, as interesting utterances of opinion and feeling, to which there would probably arise some occasion for reference. This selection from and arrangement of these articles is offered as a curious study of the attitude, temper, and purposes of the largest and most influential part of a great and enlightened nation in regard to one of the most important political movements of modern times. It is published, as its last sentences show, with no intention of putting a rougher edge upon the natural exasperation caused by the tone of the undeniably able and dextrous writers and politicians, who, to please the public for whom they wrote and spoke, opposed, ridiculed, and contemned our people and our government during the tremendous struggle for the worthy and honorable existence of our country. It would not be very easy for us to forget these efforts of our inimical kinsfolk, or indeed desirable that we should lose sight of so instructive a warning, but it will be very easy for us to forgive them. Indeed, as after 1776, and 1812, it will be much easier for us to forgive them their ill-treatment than for them to forgive us our success. But it may be well for us to cast one reflective glance upon this subject as we pass on to the great work before us, thinking the while of our country (in the words of Mr. Lowell's *Ode in commemoration of the Living and Dead Soldiers of Harvard University*, which reaches the present writer opportunely just as these pages are going to press,)

> "No challenge sends she to the elder world
> That looked askance and hated; a light scorn
> Plays on her mouth as round her mighty knees
> She calls her children back, and waits the morn
> Of nobler day, enthroned between her subject seas."

REBEL BRAG AND BRITISH BLUSTER.

INTRODUCTION.

When the people of the late Slave States were betrayed and incited by a selfish and ambitious oligarchy into undertaking the destruction of our Republic, they appealed directly to the interests, the fears and the prejudices of the governing classes of Great Britain for countenance and aid in their rebellion. Consequently, the Government and the people of the Free States looked with interest to see what attitude would be assumed in regard to the coming contest by that part of the British people which exercised a controlling influence upon the British Government and the British press. They knew that these people — to a certain degree at least, and in a certain way — hated slavery, and had been committed for a generation to a strong anti-slavery policy. The slaveholders of our Southern States having seceded, by their own admission, solely on account of the announced determination of the party coming into power to resist the extension of slavery into the unorganized national territory, and having declared by the mouth of the Vice President of their Confederacy that they meant to found their government upon slavery as its corner stone, it might have been reasonably expected that the moral weight of the British people would be thrown entirely with the Government of the United States and against the slaveholding insurgents. Perfect neutrality between the contending parties was of course looked for;—a neutrality as absolute as that of our government and people in all the various wars in which Great Britian has engaged during the present century, or as that which we should have observed had the people in England north of the Humber revolted, and attempted to set up a new government because they had been worsted in an election by the result of which they feared that some supposable interest of theirs had been imperilled. Not a neutrality which would begin by reducing a government with which we had long-standing treaties to the level of insurgents only a month or two in arms who were seeking to destroy it; thus insulting it and aiding them; but a real neutrality, which, neither elevating the other nor degrading the other, would aid neither, and do — just nothing. What was expected was merely that such possible moral influence as the British Government and people could exert, should be exerted in favor of an established constitutional government, the destruction of which was attempted by the enemies of freedom.

There were other reasons than those just mentioned, which seemed to warrant such expectations. The visit of the Prince of Wales to the United States had been eagerly seized as a fitting opportunity for a notably hearty and general demonstration of national good will to the mother-country, of which he was regarded as the representative; and this demonstration had not only been welcomed by the principal organs of British public opinion, but had been made the occasion of a candid confession that during previous years British authors, travelers and journalists, had indulged themselves in irritating misrepresentation and an unbecoming and insulting tone toward the people of this country. The London *Times* of November 16th, 1860, commenting in its leading columns upon the reception given in New York to the heir-apparent of the British throne, said, with a touch of frankness and generosity rare, upon this subject:

INTRODUCTION. 9

The work to be done here was one beyond the power of either soldier or diplomatist. A new relation had to be established between two of the greatest Empires in the world, members of the same family, heirs of the same grand traditions, the same historical names, the same language, religion, and laws. For near a century the gulf of a bloody schism has gaped between them, and the triumph of success on the one side has been met with the sneers of disappointed dominion on the other. They have forgotten in the petty resentments of the hour that we are their elder brothers and fathers, and we have forgotten that they are but our young kinsmen, and that what is amiss in them must come of our breeding. Every tourist has had his fling at their freedom of manners, their laxity of opinion, and the stern reaction of their Puritan theology. Men who could but know but little of their own country, and its still undigested heptarchy of dialects and manners, have made their sport of phrases and usages to be found in full vogue within six hours of this metropolis. . . . He (the Prince of Wales,) has expressed to America the true sentiment of every British heart to that great cognate nation. There is none in which we are so interested, none the success and glory of which we hear with such unmixed satisfaction, none with which we so identify ourselves. The Prince of Wales, while showing the feelings of a true born Englishman, has elicited the feelings of every true born American, and so brought the two face to face and made them feel that they are brothers.

Very charming this, if it had only lasted; but how quickly was it all to change!

It was also remembered that the only discourtesy the Prince met with here was shown him in a slave State, and that he turned away from Richmond shaking, in a princely fashion, its dust from his princely feet.

Again, it could not be forgotten that when Great Britain appeared before the world in the Crimean war as the antagonist of the great Muscovite empire which, however foreign its domestic feeling to the sympathies of the people of the Free States, had still that claim upon our regard which is given by a constant attitude of consideration and respect, by which it was distinguished from its opponents, the mass of our people had manifested a lively interest in the success of the arms of the allies one of whom represented our blood and, in a greater measure than any other, our principles of government, and the other a people with which we had ourselves been in former years on terms of close alliance. These are not after thoughts. In the first year of the war these considerations were thus substantially set forth in the special correspondence of one of the principal journals of the United States — the New York *Times*.

When Great Britian and France went to war eight years ago with Russia, in order to check that semi-civilized power in its career of conquest, the almost universal sentiment in that portion of this country which is now loyal to the Union was in cordial sympathy with the former, and their earnest prayers went up for the overthrow of the armies of the Muscovite despot. There were a few exceptions to this general unanimity, but I can now remember only the *Tribune* as occupying that position, and I believe that its peculiar, not to say eccentric views, met with little sympathy among Northern men.* At the South, however, the senti-

---

* The sympathy which we felt for these brave, patient British soldiers found fitting utterance in these lines, written by one of our most widely known authors, upon a touching incident in the siege of Sevastopol.

SONGS OF THE CAMP.
BY BAYARD TAYLOR.
Air,— The girls I left behind me.

"Give us a song!" the soldiers cried,
　The outer trenches guarding,
When the heated gun of the camp allied
　Grew weary of bombarding.

The dark Redan, in silent scoff,
　Lay, grim and threatening, under,
And the tawny mouth of the Malakoff
　No longer belched its thunder.

There was a pause. The guardman said
" We storm the forts to-morrow;
Sing while we may, another day
　Will bring enough of sorrow."

They lay along the battery's side
　Below the smoking cannon —
Brave hearts from Severn and from Clyde,
　And from the banks of Shannon.

They sang of love and not of fame —
　Forgot was Britain's glory.
Each heart recalled a different name,
　But all sang — " Annie Laurie."

ment was almost as universally in favor of the barbaric despotism which then tolerated Slavery, and this circumstance, in fact, constituted the real bond of sympathy. The organ of Mr. Pierce's administration — the Washington *Union* — took strong ground in favor of the Russian cause in the very outset of the contest. That paper was then edited nominally by an old soldier from Tennessee, General Armstrong, but really by Roger A. Pryor, a fire-eating Virginian. The course of the organ, in siding with Russia, was deemed extraordinary, and gave such offence to Northern sentiment that it was found necessary to get rid of the impracticable sympathizer with Russian despotism, and he was disposed of by being appointed as Minister or Consul to Greece. But the slavery controversy waxed warmer every day, and the exactions of the Southern democracy upon its Northern allies grew apace, until not only the official organ, but the whole Southern and a portion of the Northern Democratic press, took ground in favor of Russia as the power of kindred principles which fought for the spread of despotism and slavery. All sorts of specious charges were urged against Great Britain and France, based on affected fears of their ambitious designs, but the real moving cause, as everybody knew, was the affinity which exists between the propagandists of black slavery, and what they regarded as the propagandists of white slavery.

Again, when four years ago, Great Britain was threatened with the loss of her most considerable possession, the fruit of a century of wars and intrigues, the American heart — or I should say

---

  Voice after voice caught up the song,
   Until its tender passion
  Rose like an anthem, rich and strong —
   Their battle eve confession.

  Dear girl — her name he dared not speak —
   Yet, as the song grew louder,
  Something upon the soldier's cheek
   Washed off the stains of powder.

  Beyond the darkening ocean burned
   The bloody sunset's embers,
  While the Crimean valleys learned
   How English love remembers.

  And Irish Nora's eyes are dim
   For a singer, dumb and gory!
  And English Mary mourns for him
   Who sang of "Annie Laurie."

  Ah! soldiers, to your honored rest
   Your truth and valor bearing:
  The bravest are the tenderest —
   The loving are the daring!

rather, the Northern, and now loyal American heart — went forth in sympathy with their kinsmen. We could not justify the means resorted to by the Government of Great Britain in acquiring possession of India, nor the administration which had been accorded to that barbarous people, but it was generally felt that the East Indians, a semi-barbarous people, accustomed for ages to the misrule of local and warring despots, and to the benumbing influence of frightful superstitions, were better off, and in a more hopeful way of progress under British rule than under that of their native despots. This consideration, coupled with our kind wishes for the people from whom we sprung, caused a general sympathy with the British nation, and a general rejoicing at the suppression of the rebellion. The South, on the contrary, manifested a deal of sympathy with the Sepoys. Great Britian had abolished slavery in the West Indies; she contained Exeter Hall, and her priests and nobles feasted and honored the authoress of *Uncle Tom's Cabin*, and refused to surrender fugitive slaves. These were reasons sufficient to turn the sympathies of all Pro-slavery men, North and South, in favor of the Sepoys.*

So much for the past. At length the party in this country with which all Britain professed to sympathize — the party of freedom and justice, of civilization and humanity, of peace with Great Britain and all the world — the party hostile to slavery extension, the slave-trade and fillibustering — triumphed in an election. It installed a President of its choice, and had the control of one branch of Congress. But the champions of the slave-trade, of slavery extension and of fillibustering, revolt. They will not submit to a "Black Republican" president, though fairly elected, and they plunder the arsenals and armories of the government located among them, in order to arm their fellow-citizens for the destruction of the Union. What does slavery-hating England do in this crisis of the American Government? Does she reciprocate our kind sympathies, bestowed during the Russian and Sepoy wars? Does she frown indignantly upon the attempt to build

---

* In the *Atlantic Monthly* Oliver Wendell Holmes thus quaintly expresses our feeling upon this subject:

"Who was that person that was so absurd some time since for saying that in the conflict of two races our sympathies naturally go with the higher? No matter who he was. Now look what is going on in India, — a white, superior 'Caucasian' race against a dark skinned but still inferior 'Caucasian' race, — and where are English and American sympathies? We can't stop to settle all the doubtful questions. . . . . The India mail brings stories of women and children outraged and murdered. The royal stronghold is in the hands of the babe-killers. England takes down the map of the world which she has girdled with empire, and makes a correction, thus: ~~DELHI~~, *dele*. The civilized world says, Amen."

The British people seemed to set at naught that which Taylor and Holmes expressed. Well, if they are content, so are we.

up a great Confedaracy upon the basis of a revival of the slave-trade, the extension of slavery by fillibustering, and the perpetration of negro bondage? Yes! she does for a while affect these virtues. She does mention a little, through her *Times* and other journals, her Russells and Palmerstons, about the horrors of slavery and the beauties of freedom; but she, at the same time, perfidiously keeps one ear open to the traitors, and tells them, *sub rosa*, to persevere for a few months, until Great Britain will feel justified in acknowledging their independence. This is briefly and substantially the history of British treatment of the American rebellion. It has been a history of hypocrisy and duplicity — of affected concern for the interests of freedom and humanity, but of real concern for the interests of cotton-spinning and commerce.

The overthrow of the slaveholding rebellion will place mother England in a most unenviable attitude. She will have forfeited for a generation the confidence and respect of the American people and government, and have steeped herself in the guilt of a conspiracy to overthrow a free Constitution, in order to set up one whose " being, end and aim " is the extension and perpetuation of slavery and the slave-trade. This generation must pass away before this crime against humanity can be forgotten.

As late as March 2d, 1861, *Punch*, which is always on the side of freedom and constitutional government when it is not its interest to be on that of slavery and despotism — taking the natural and traditional British view of slavery and slave holding, and of resistance to lawful authority under a free government, spoke as follows on occasion of one step in the secession movement:

We see that Louisiana has seceded from the American Union in a manner equally disgusting and ridiculous. Despatches from Baton Rouge contain the particulars of this absurb proceeding. The debate in the Convention on the question of secession having closed, we are told, a vote was ordered, and:—
" The Galleries and lobbies were intensely crowded, and a death-like silence prevailed. On the call of the roll, many members were in tears."
Who were the weepers? A numerous minority in the Louisiana Convention, bewailing the folly which the majority was about to perpetrate? Not so; for the vote having been announced, the Ayes turned out to be 113, and the Nays 17. The weeping members were therefore Secessionists—slave-owners, slave-drivers—and about what then were these ruffians blubbering? We can only suppose either that their tears were those of maudlin mournfulness, or drunkenness, or proceeded from the fountain of doleful hypocrisy.

That the latter was the source of these crocodiles' or alligators' tears, is very decidedly indicated by what follows:—

"Capt. Allen then entered the Convention with a Pelican flag, accompanied by Governor Moore and staff, and put the flag in the hands of the President, amid tremendous excitement.

"A solemn prayer was then offered, and a hundred guns fired."

Having agreed in an act of treason towards their common country, in pursuance of a brutal determination to persist in oppressing their fellow-men; having renounced their allegiance to the American Union, to the intent of persevering in the violation of their duty towards their neighbour, these snivelling professors of a rascally piety go down on their knees and pray. Hideous devotion! Praying and weeping as they were, surely every drop that trickled from their turned-up eyes down their snuffling noses, must have looked black in the light of Heaven. Angelic chemistry has perhaps turned those tears to jet, and keeps them for a curiosity. Unpleasant humbugs! The odour of their sanctimony grievously offends the moral nose.

The finishing touch to the character of these brutes is supplied by the following account of an atrocity narrated in a despatch dated at Washington:—

"Information was received by the Government this morning, from the Collector at New Orleans, stating that the barracks about two miles below New Orleans, now occupied as a Marine Hospital, were taken possession of on the 11th instant by Captain Bradford, of the State Infantry, in the name of the State of Louisiana. There were 216 invalids and convalescent patients in the hospital at the time it was seized. The collector of customs was required to immediately remove the patients who were convalescent, and those who were confined to their beds, as soon as practicable. This action is regarded by the Government as most outrageous and inhuman."

The hospital was seized, and the patients were turned out of it in order that it might be occupied as a barrack by the state troops of Louisiana, levied on behalf of slavery and rebellion. Secretary Dix denounces this deed as "an act of outrageous barbarity, disgraceful to any age or country." But what are the savage secessionist slave-owners of Louisiana but barbarians?

"Ruffians," "maudlin mournfulness or doleful hypocrisy," "crocodiles' tears," "an act of treason toward their common country in pursuance of a brutal determination to persist in oppressing their fellow-men," "snivelling professors of a rascally piety," "hideous devotion," "snuffling noses," "unpleasant humbugs," "brutes," "barbarians." What that was ever said by the coarsest and most indiscreet of loyal anti-slavery journals approached *Punch's* vituperation of the insurgent slave-holders? But there is no more sensitive meter of British public feeling than this mercurial mountebank, and we shall hereafter see how quietly he adapted himself to the change of moral atmosphere round him, when John Bull got the idea in his head that at last there was a chance for the destruction of the Great Republic.

That at first the organs of British public opinion took the right position in reference to the rebellion, and did not abandon it until they were tempted by the reflection, which came with time and in consequence of the suggestion of rebel emissaries, that if encouraged and nursed, the rebellion might divide the power of the United States, will be brought to mind by the following extracts from the London *Times* and *Saturday Review*.

We are glad to think that the march of slavery and the domineering tone which its advocates were beginning to assume have at length been arrested and silenced. We rejoice that a vast community of our own race has at length given an authoritative expression to sentiments which are entertained by every one in this country.—*Times*, Nov. 21, 1860.

Should South Carolina, Georgia and the adjacent states, separate themselves permanently from the Federation, constituting themselves a new nation, with their own army, navy, foreign representatives, and all the appanage of independence, then the whole series of American politicians will have been in the wrong, and *this journal, which has always declared such an event to be impossible*, will have been in the wrong with them.—*Times*, Nov. 26, 1860.

Of one thing the Democrats may well be assured — that the character and prestige of the United States in the eyes of Europe depend on their Federal Union . . . Let there be no mistake as to English public opinion on this subject. If we have paid a sincere homage to the rising greatness of America, it has not been to that which the Southerners are so anxious to conserve, but to that which they are striving to destroy. All that is noble and venerable in the United States is associated with the Federal Constitution. It is not the demonstration of Southern ruffianism in Congress, or the fillibustering aggression of the South,— from Mexican aggression down to the Fugitive Slave Law or the Dred Scott decision, or the Kansas-Nebraska Act — it is not these or any other triumph of

Democratic insolence during their ascendency of half a century that has commanded the sympathy and admiration of Europe. . . But if this rough sparring [the threats of secession] should by any chance be carried too far, and the threat uttered in jest or earnest should be repeated in earnest, and lead to bloodshed, it is some comfort that the aggressor will not be the strong party. Mr. Lincoln will in that case command a majority in Congress, and will carry with him the support of all those who, however tolerant of slavery, will not acquiesce in its becoming the basis of an illegal and hostile Confederacy.—*Times*, Nov. 29, 1860.

It is evident, in short, that the dissolution of the United States, so far from being hailed as a profitable transaction, will be lamented in this country as the premature failure of a great experiment, and as a probable source of grave diplomatic embarrassment.—*Saturday Review*, Dec. 29, 1860.

It is in truth absolutely certain that any policy will miscarry, which assumes that England can be coaxed or bribed into a connivance at the extension of slavery.—*Saturday Review*, Dec. 29, 1860.

This was the attitude in the early stages of the rebellion, of that part of the British people which has a voice in public affairs. What was that of the secessionists themselves? We all remember the boast of Mr. Pope Walker, the insurgent "Secretary of War" at Montgomery, the day of the surrender of Fort Sumter,—"No man can tell where the war commenced this day will end; but I will prophesy that the flag which now flaunts the breeze here, will float over the dome of their old capitol at Washington, before the first of May. Let them try Southern chivalry, and test the extent of Southern resources, and it may float eventually over Faneuil Hall itself." But we have more authoritative statements of higher expectations and more definite purposes than these. Mr. Jefferson Davis, speaking at Stevenson, Alabama, in February, 1861, thus announced the speedily coming triumph of the rebellion, and the means by which it was to be accomplished.

"Your border states will gladly come into the Southern Confederacy within sixty days, as we will be your only friends. *Eng-*

land will recognise us, and a glorious future is before us, *the grass will grow in Northern cities,* where the pavements have been worn by the tread of commerce. *We will carry war where it is easy to advance — where food for the sword and the torch await the armies in the densely populated cities;* and though the enemy may come and spoil our crops we can raise them as before; while they cannot rear the cities which it took years of industry and millions of money to build."

So much from the President of the Confederate States of America. The leading journal of this " Confederacy " thus discoursed and prophesied :

It is a good maxim " not to quarrel with one's bread and butter," and one which *the North will remember to its sorrow long ere its war upon the South is ended.* It has no idea yet of the extent of its dependence upon the South, and upon slaveholding countries south of us. Cotton is king, but not the only king. Sugar, molasses, rice, tobacco and many other southern products, are kings and petty princes. *The North cannot subsist without them,* yet she is about to excite a system of privateering that will cut up her commerce, and *if it does not starve her, will force her to live upon half allowance.* She can't live on leather long, and neither her shoes or other manufactures will find a market after war is fully entered into.

* * * * * * *

The north-eastern states of America are situated, as regards trade and subsistence, just as are western and southern Europe. Their soil, in its present impoverished condition, *could not be made to produce food and clothing to sustain their population.* They might live without cotton, or tea, or coffee, or rice, or sugar, or spices, molasses, or tobacco, if they had sufficient breadth of soil on which to produce substitutes for these articles; but this they have not. They have begun to blockade the whole southern coast. *If they succeed, the South may nevertheless live as comfortably and luxuriously within itself as if it enjoyed the trade and commerce of the world.*

* * * * * * *

A ten years' successful blockade of the north-eastern states (we mean an exclusion from the markets of the world) would starve one half of their population and impoverish the other half. Northern wealth is a very ticklish concern. Without foreign trade it would take to itself wings and fly off; or, if it remained at home, would cease to have any value. Without trade, her factories, her ships, her stores, her cities and her moneyed capital, would be valueless — would cease to constitute wealth. *Her poverty is indigenous — her riches cosmopolitan.* If she continues to war upon the South, her moneyed capital and her capital employed in trade and manufactures will seek investment in other countries. Then she will have nothing but *her sterile soil and her millions of paupers. War can do us no serious injury, but will be sure to ruin her.* The slave population of the South can support in comfort four times as many people as we have within our confines. We can keep a million of men under arms and never suffer for want of comfortable food and clothing. Slaveholding begets and fosters the war spirit. After a while the master race begins to think its whole business is to fight, whilst the inferior race does the labor. This is a division of labor which we do not altogether admire and approve; but it is well for us and for our enemies to know that it is not an unnatural one, nor has it been an unusual one. Among the most polished and civilized nations of antiquity this was the normal and approved condition of things.

The North will be at a loss to select its soldiery. Her factory hands and her farmers know little about guns, and would take a long time to learn to stand fire, however expert they be at carrying Wide Awake lanterns. Hannibal did once whip a Roman army, by tying fodder to the tails and horns of a drove of oxen, setting fire to the fodder and driving the oxen in among the Romans. *We doubt very much whether the Wide Awakes could be driven by their officers in among our Southern troops, and we know they will never lead them in.*

Then, again, if the Northern factory hands and farmers are carried to the wars, who will produce food and clothing? *War will disorganize the industry of the North; it can have little effect upon ours.*—*Richmond Examiner*, April 16th, 1861.

With the course of events during the war fresh in our memories, and the present condition of the revolted states before our eyes, it is almost impossible to believe that men having a moderate degree of that sense which is common to mankind, could deliberately utter such boastful nonsense. But the judgment of these men had been self-perverted for a generation by the endeavor to maintain the justice of an institution at variance with the spirit of civilization and christianity; and they were given over to delusions. Witness this testimony of a writer, Mr. Russell, whose testimony as to matters of fact is as good as can be offered:

THE STATE OF SOUTH CAROLINA.

Nothing I could say can be worth one fact which has forced itself upon my mind in reference to the sentiments which prevail among the gentlemen of this State. I have been among them for several days. I have visited their plantations, I have conversed with them freely and fully, and I have enjoyed that frank, courteous, and graceful intercourse which constitutes an irresistible charm of their society. From all quarters has come to my ears the echoes of the same voice; it may be feigned, but there is no discord in the note, and it sounds in wonderful strength and monotony all over the country. Shades of George III., of North, of Johnson, of all who contended against the great rebellion which tore these colonies from England, can you hear the chorus which rings through the State of Marion, Sumpter, and Pinckney, and not clap your ghostly hands in triumph? That voice says *"If we could only get one of the Royal race of England to rule over us, we should be content."* Let there be no misconception on this point. That sentiment, varied in a hundred ways, has been repeated to me over and over again. There is a general admission that the means to such an end are wanting, and that the desire cannot be gratified. But the admiration for monarchical institutions on the English model, for privileged classes, and for a landed aristocracy and gentry, is undisguised and apparently genuine. With the pride of having achieved their independence is mingled in the South Carolinians' heart a strange regret at the result and consequences, and many are they who "would go back to-morrow if we could."— *Special Correspondence of the London Times*, April 30, 1861.

But between the writing of the above paragraph and that which follows, Mr. Russel had gone from South Carolina to Georgia. The uprising at the North, in response to the President's proclamation, had caused some of the Southern people to open their eyes — at least with astonishment. The consequence was a change of tone, which the British correspondent thus records:

May day was so well kept yesterday that the exhausted editors cannot "bring out" their papers, and consequently there is no news; but there is, nevertheless, much to be said concerning "*Our* President's" message, and there is a suddenness of admiration for pacific tendencies which can with difficulty be accounted for, unless the news from the North these last few days has something to do with it. *Not a word now about an instant march on Washington! No more threats to seize on Faneuil Hall!* The Georgians are by no means so keen as the Carolinians on their border — nay, they are not so belligerent to-day as they were a week ago. Mr. Jefferson Davis' message is praised for its "moderation," and for other qualities which were by no means in such favor while the Sumter fever was at its height. Men look grave and talk about the interference of England and France, which "cannot allow this thing to go on." *But the change which has come over them is unmistakable, and the best men begin to look grave. As for me, I must prepare to open my lines of retreat — my communications are in danger.*—Special Correspondence of the London Times, May 2, 1861.

While the Secessionists were bragging and threatening as we have seen, what was the tone of the people of the loyal States? It was as unlike as their principles were, to that of the insurgent slave-holders. A careful search through the leading newspapers published north of the Potomac discovers an earnest but somewhat subdued assertion of faith in the Republic, and devotion to its principles and its flag, but no boast of prowess, no blatant prediction of swift and triumphant success. From this as from every statement creditable to the press of the United States, there must of course be excepted one notorious paper, which has gained its notoriety only by pandering to the worst tastes and passions of the ignorant foreign population of New York, and the prurient curiosity of its native inhabitants, and which, having been a supporter of the seceders even after the bombardment of Sumter, changed face between two days, and, always a braggart, endeavored to beget confidence in its new-born loyalty by its extravagant boastfulness. But there is more than this negative evidence of the moderate pretensions of the loyal people amid all their confidence and devotion. The New York *Times*, with the approval of the whole community, Irishmen and rowdies excepted, thus rebuked the correspondent of a leading London paper for a pretentious and boastful tone which was felt to be unbecoming and regarded as misrepresenting the country:

ZEAL WITHOUT DISCRETION.

The London *Daily News* has distinguished itself from the mass of English newspapers no less by the knowledge of American affairs which it has shown in the present crisis, than by its sympathy with the cause of constitutional liberty and freedom. But it has a correspondent who signs himself "Americus," who harms the cause he advocates by exhibiting in their most objectionable forms the overweening self-confidence and the disposition to bluster which the leading British journals most unjustly attribute, as a characteristic trait, to Americans in general, and to American journalists in particular. This will be seen by the following extract from a late letter :

" From these statements it is evident enough that the Confederate States, so far from being able to sustain their position against the National Government, *have not ability to maintain even their local supremacy*, and those British statesmen who are looking forward to an early opportunity for recognizing the independence of the seceders, might as well pause in their policy until they ascertain that they are even tolerably unanimous among themselves. As sure as there is a sun in the heavens the rebellion will be put down. *In sixty days Virginia will be all right again.* North Carolina and Georgia really take no active part with the Confederates. Arkansas is again in a shiver of uncertainty, and before the year is out British ships will be loading in the Southern ports and taking their clearances from United States Custom Houses. Your government, therefore, will do well to avoid any premature action, *and had better 'proceed no further with this business.' If they do, there will be a sorry sight.*

" *One single false step on the part of your Administration will produce the entire loss of your trade.* While I am now writing, patriotic Home Leagues are organizing for the purpose of discouraging the wear, purchase and use of all British manufactures in the Northern and Western States. *Not a dollar's worth of your fabric will be consumed among us, if you recognize the Southern Confederacy.* This is no threat or thought of mine. It is a simple and stubborn fact, and is the first movement contemplated as retaliatory for any hasty recognition."

If this were a fair sample of the style or the feeling of the representative men of this country, the judgment passed upon us by the London papers would be fully justified.

THE "TRENT" AFFAIR.

The disgraceful and unreasonable panic by which the well fought and nearly won battle of Bull Run was finally lost, gave great encouragement to hopes already excited on both sides of the water, and was made the occasion of much Rebel brag and British bluster which need not be particularly noticed here; and ere long the ill-advised, but not unnatural step of Captain Wilkes afforded the British enemies of the United States a favorable opportunity, which they did not neglect, of putting the bad feeling and prejudice already existing among their countrymen to use against our government, and of arousing in those who had previously been indifferent a resentment, which although it had no just foundation, was as natural as the feeling of satisfaction which Captain Wilkes's act first awakened in this country. We all remembered the action of the British government toward us upon the same subject, which led to the war of 1812—14; and that although the war was brought to a close by the treaty of Ghent, the British Government had not withdrawn their claim to take British subjects from under our flag upon the high sea, or to stop and search even our vessels of war for that purpose. That was our last information as to British policy upon this subject. Therefore, although it is now well known that had Captain Wilkes had an opportunity of communicating with his government he would not have taken the Rebel Commissioners out of the Trent, every man of us felt at first a certain satisfaction in knowing that Great Britain had had her own chalice put to her lips by one of our naval commanders. We know that whether the act was in itself justifiable or not, Great Britain had no right to complain of it, and especially at our hand. Of this there is the best possible evidence in the following paragraph from a leading article in the London *Times*, published immediately upon the arrival of the news in England.

It requires a strong effort of self-restraint to discuss with coolness the intelligence we publish to-day. . . . Unwelcome as the truth may be, it is nevertheless a truth that *we have ourselves established a system of international law which now tells against us.* In high-handed and almost despotic manner we have in former days [but within the memory of many yet living] claimed privileges over neutrals which have at different times banded all the maritime powers of the world against us. We have insisted upon stopping ships of war of neutral nations and taking British subjects out of them. . . . We have been the strenuous asserters of the rights of belligerents over neutrals; and the decisions of our courts of law *as they must now be cited by our law-officers* have been in conformity to those unreasonable claims which have called into being confederacies, and aroused neutrals against us, and which have always been modified in practice when we were not supreme in dominion at sea." — *Times*, Oct. 28, 1861.

The same just and sensible view of the case was taken two months later by that eminent scholar and publicist, Professor Newman, in the following letter which appeared in the London *Star:*

To the Editor of the " Star and Dial." SIR,—Your correspondent " Irenieus," of January 1, deprecates our making " excuses for Captain Wilkes and his applauding countrymen." I think he confounds excuses with justifications. He further says that " unless America can assume at once the character of belligerent and non-belligerent, she cannot obtain the least excuse for her proceedings from anything that England has done." He surely forgets that we recently fought two wars with China (Lord Palmerston being then, as now, Prime Minister,) without any declaration of war: and when some persons raised an outcry that to do so was to be guilty of piracy, the *Times* replied, that to become belligerent would be highly inconvenient to our merchants, who would then no longer be at liberty to carry on commerce with " the enemy." England then chose to be simultaneously belligerent and non-belligerent; and is without the shadow of an excuse for being now so squeamish on the question of " belligerent rights," as distinct from moral rights and natural proprieties.

> *The act of Captain Wilkes, and the liberties taken by our ships against the Americans in our war with Napoleon, appear to me alike unjustifiable and unendurable.* No one has a right to expect nations to regulate their feelings by the pettifogging of arbitary rules, which have been made by the powerful to suit their own convenience. Governments, indeed, ought not rudely to violate precedent, but President Lincoln has not yet taken any of the liberties which our Chinese wars assumed. Of course, he cannot admit that the Southerners are not rebels. In a military sense, he is evidently conceding to them belligerent rights, which is the obvious dictate of morality whenever rebels are strong enough to meet you in the field; although we in the late Indian war had not virtue nor wisdom to understand this. But in no civil sense will he concede that they have belligerent rights. *If they are beaten in the war, of course their leaders will be visited with legal penalties, such as are necessary to prevent a repetition of their offence.* And in this sense, I apprehend, nothing is more reasonable than that the North should be simultaneously belligerent and non-belligerent. But it can gain no moral rights, as against neutrals, by declaring itself to be one or other. The Northerners, naturally enough, are trying to justify Captain Wilkes's act by our precedents. The precedents do not perfectly tally to a lawyer's mind, *but they are as like as two peas to a moral view,* which is the only view which masses of men can take. Hence, I conclude, we have to pull the beam out of our own eye first, and then may see more clearly to pull out the mote from our brother's eye.

This was, we see, as inevitably it must have been, the verdict of every man of whatever country, who was sufficiently well informed to know the relations of the British to that of the United States upon this subject, and sufficiently candid to form his judgment without prejudice or passion. But on second thoughts it was seen by our enemies that here was an opportunity of humiliating the Republic, or of bringing a second and, it was supposed, a certainly destructive war upon its hands, which was too good to be let slip. Whereupon there was an outbreak of denunciation and of demand for satisfaction, which is still fresh in the world's memory, and of which the following paragraph is a very mild specimen:

> This event, which has kindled all the honest blood of England, throws us back almost to the days of 1812. We fancy we see the Chesapeake coming out again, with a cask full of handcuffs on her deck, to fight the old Shannon, which made a wreck of her. The quarrel of that epoch arose out of a question not dissimilar to that

which our Foreign Secretary is now challenged to unravel. Government, of course, must wait for further details; but whatever may be said, nothing can explain away the necessity for reparation and apology. If Captain Wilkes and Lieutenant Fairfax acted without instructions they must be reprimanded and dismissed from the navy. We must have the Commissioners given up. We must have atonement for that shot and that shell fired without notice at a steamer conveying the Royal Mail, in charge of a Queen's officer. If there are persons who believe that Englishmen will be satisfied with less, they are pitiably mistaken. We made war in China for the sake of a fishing-boat; we may, at least, then, dare to protest when our national flag has been virtually hauled down upon the high seas. The Federals have a right to ransack our ocean steamers! The doctrine is monstrous."

Certainly, because this time it was your ox that had gored my bull.

What was the attitude of the people of this country? It was one of unmixed satisfaction that Great Britain had been at last made to feel, and to feel at our hands, what it was to have *her* ships stopped upon the high seas, that the subjects of another government might be taken from them, while at the same time there was a determination among all sober and considerate people — in a word, among the great mass of our citizens who control the government, to give up the Rebel Commissioners should the British Government demand them, and should that demand be found to be a proper one. This was shown by the dispatch upon the subject sent immediately by Mr. Seward to our minister at London, before we had any intimation of the manner in which the news of the seizure was received by the British people.

And the New York *Times* thus commented upon the resolutions of the House of Representatives complimenting Captain Wilkes:

In thus putting on record a formal approval of an act which has called forth universal public satisfaction, there is, of course, no intention to prejudge a case on which neither our own nor the British Government has yet pronounced an opinion, and which is now properly a matter of diplomacy alone. We all liked the bold deed, and we liked it all the better because it seemed to be perfectly justified by the principles and precedents of international law. Should it *not* be so justified, there can be no hesitation as to the course to be pursued; however gratifying the seizure of the rebel ambassadors may have been, it is not worth the sacrifice of a single principle of the public morality of nations.

Upon this passage a British journal of repute, the *Manchester Guardian*, well remarked as follows, December 17th, 1861:

If this be really the lofty and candid spirit in which the action of Congress and other manifestations of public opinion are regarded by those whose voice will be final, there is no reason yet for despairing of a pacific solution of the question. We wait, surely not in confidence, but in hope.

We did not think this spirit particularly "lofty;" it was simple good faith and common sense; just what Mr. Seward meant when he wrote his first dispatch immediately on the arrival of the news in this country, of which dispatch the British public at this time had been permitted to know nothing. There was a confident tone here, upon the subject, which was taken merely upon the assumption that John Bull would not have the face to ask us — of all nations — to give up our own citizens taken from one of his ships. But we overrated both Brother John's consistency and his modesty.

But in spite of these demonstrations, it was determined that so good an opportunity to humiliate our country or to aid in its disruption must not be lost. Mr. Seward's dispatch was not communicated to the public through Parliament, and the expressions of willingness to give up Messrs. Slidell and Mason were for a time passed by. Whatever was done upon the subject here was misrepresented or carped at. The Saturday *Review* of December 7th, said: —

If Mr. Lincoln has been prudent enough to pass over in silence the capture of the Southern Commissioners, he may still be at liberty to comply with the requisitions of international law. The Senate, or its Committee on Foreign Relations, may perhaps waive its concurrent authority; or, if it has the wisdom and patriotism to share the responsibility of a just concession, it may protect the Executive against the unpopularity which might otherwise be incurred by the surrender of the prisoners.

Well, Mr. Lincoln *was* " prudent enough " to pass the subject over in silence ; whereupon the London *Times* spoke thus, December 17th :

> It is not easy to see why Mr. Lincoln should have omitted from his speech all notice of the case of the Trent. If he means to give up the persons illegally seized, one would have thought it no unwise precaution to prepare the public mind for such a decision. If he means to keep them, we cannot understand why he does not grasp at all the popularity that is to be had in exchange for present war and future ruin, instead of allowing it to be picked up by obscure members of Congress embarking in a contest whether the transcendent merits of Commodore Wilkes would be best rewarded by thanks or by a gold medal.

Mr. Lincoln was to be found fault with and sneered at all the same, speaking or silent. This was not all. When it became too plain to be longer concealed that the rebel commissioners would be restored to British protection, and that the longed-for opportunity was lost although the very articles from the New York *Times* above quoted had been published in some of the London papers, the willingness to make the restoration was attributed to fear excited by hostile proceedings, of which nothing could have been known until long after Mr. Seward's dispatch was written, and sometime after the declarations in question were made in our most respectable and influential papers. The mischief-makers thus presented this view of the case :

> The prospects of peace have improved, for the Americans have been startled into decorum and moderation. The British demand for redress acted upon an excitable people like a cold douche on a drunkard, producing first irritation, then bewilderment, and then a return to sober sense. Up to the 16th of December, when they

had heard only of English excitement, the papers were still full of elation, [Will it be believed, the article from the N. Y. *Times*, above quoted, was *published in England* on the 17th of December, and the first intimation of a demand for the commissioners and of warlike preparation reached this country on the 16th of that month,] fully convinced that remonstrance would be confined to an article in the *Times* or a speech in the House of Commons. . . Further evidence, however, dispelled many of these illusions. The rapid collection of transports, the despatch of the troops to Canada, the order to the Guards to be ready for active service, the seizure of saltpetre, the addresses of the Naval reserve, and, above all, the letters sent from influential Americans in London, convinced all men not wilfully deaf, that England was roused at last, and that the only alternative was a just conciliation or war. Then at last the politicians began to reflect, to take stock, as it were, of their position, to remember that whatever the other results of a maritime war, it must at least cost them the South. The papers became suddenly decent.—*Saturday Review*, Jan. 4th, 1862.

Never for a moment did the people or the Government of America show a symptom of repenting the unjust act of Captain Wilkes. When the first utterances of the English journals after news of the outrage came to hand, their tone of moderation was falsely interpreted into a recognition of the justice of Captain Wilkes's proceeding. Never till America heard that the ink with which Earl Russell's peremptory despatches were written was not dry before all the energies of our Government were directed to hostile preparations, did the public opinion of the United States waver. But it did waver *then*. When troops were ordered to Canada—when ship after ship was commissioned to carry out men and military stores for the defence of the Canadian frontier—when it was evident that the British lion was thoroughly roused from the inaction of mingled prudence and contempt, *then* the tone of the New York press became moderate; *then* the popular feeling against giving up the Commissioners began to subside; *then* people began to think that the Federal Government, if the commands of the British Government were couched in moderate language—your Yankee loves moderate language—would be complied with; and *then* the House of Representatives, which, but a few days before, had passed a vote of thanks to Captain Wilkes, sat down, like ancient Pistol, to eat the leek it had insultingly brandished in our faces. —*Morning Chronicle* of Jan. 2, 1862.

The Trent affair was settled, and passed quietly into history, not by the reprimand and dismissal of Captain Wilkes and Lieutenant Fairfax, not by the reparation and apology which were so loudly clamored for and pronounced to be indispensable; because it was felt that Great Britain had no reasonable pretence to any such atonement, but by a simple returning of the Rebels to British protection, in accordance with principles of international intercourse which the government of the United States had maintained from the begining, and as to Great Britain's self-confessed sudden conversion to which we could not at that time prudently take exception. The record upon this subject begins, as we have seen, with a confession from the London *Times* that Great Britain herself had established a system of international law which in this matter told against them; it closes, after all the vituperation of our lawlessness and insolence, in which the *Saturday Review* bore a conspicuous part, by the following confession by that paper made two years later, surrounded with more abuse, like a bitter pill with sweet-meats, that the right of the question was not clearly on the British side, even to British eyes, until after a curious search for it.

(From the *Saturday Review* of Nov. 12, 1864.)

As the haughty claim to absolute dominion throughout the North American Continent [which was never set up] never went beyond words, those European countries to whom it was addressed as an insult treated it with the indifference which it deserved; but the same spirit of defiance of all legal and conventional restraints has more than once displayed itself on the boundaries of our own colonies, and was no doubt the chief inducement to the ill-fated experiment on our forbearance which ended in the surrender of the prisoners taken from the *Trent*. But in that case the offended Power was England, and *it must in fairness be added that the outrage was not so glaringly in excess of belligerent rights as to be recognised in its true character until after a careful study of precedents and legal authorities.*

IMPOSSIBILITY OF PUTTING DOWN THE REBELLION.

From the very earliest stages of the war the great theme of all the wiseacres in Great Britain, from John O'Groat's house to Land's End, was the impossibility, on what may be called general principles, of putting down the rebellion, and of preserving the integrity of the Republic. This was asserted in all the moods and tenses. It was predicted; it was proved. It was shown to be the only conclusion to which experienced statesmen who knew something of the past, (of which Yankees of course knew nothing,) and who had had their wits sharpened in the political collisions of the present day, could arrive. We were told about three times a week from London that all the wit and the wisdom of Europe was jeering at us and rejoicing over the ruin of the Republic, which was already regarded as accomplished. Our self-elected mentors began to give us this counsel in pure friendliness, and only for our own good, many weeks even before the Trent affair.

(From the *London Times* of Sept. 1861.)

If a clear foresight shows, and must show, *that there must be two Federations, and that on no other footing will peace ever be made*, it will be much better that it should come to pass after one year's war than after ten or twenty. It is not as if the Union or two Unions were the only alternative. As the war proceeds, no man can tell what new powers and combinations may arise, and particularly how far the Western States will endure the taxes and financial obligations necessary for the war. The advice we offer is only what the Americans have given to all the world. It is a hank of their own cotton,—a pipe of their own tobacco. Let them consider what they can do, and what neither they nor all the world can do. At present they are only giving a triumph to many a foe, for there is not a circle of old absolutist statesmen and diplomats who do not read the story of their difficulties and reverses with a bitter smile. They will hear with at least respect, perhaps with disappointment, that the North and South have agreed to part friends.

It occurs to us as barely possible that the worthy old statesmen and diplomats are now smiling on the other side of the mouth. They have not suffered the sad disappointment of seeing the North and South part friends; and as to their respect, why, "let that appear when there is no need of such vanity."

(From the *London Times* of Sept. 1861.)

The Americans rushed into the war as recklessly as any nation could have done. The Peace party among them never obtained anything like such a hearing as was accorded to our peacemakers at home. Every offer of arbitration was rejected with the fiercest contempt. They are conducting their war with such incredible prodigality that observers used to the extravagance of camps and campaigning are astounded at the spectacle, and, to complete the picture, they are providing for this enormous outlay in the most improvident and costly fashion. *Being unwilling to tax themselves, they resort to borrowing, and are raising loans at a rate which will soon make their National Debt one of the heaviest in the world.* We can only hope, indeed, that a policy so recklessly adopted, may soon bring with it, as an unavoidable consequence, the termination of the strife. If financial embarrassments should furnish the surest road to peace, the sooner they are experienced the better. We can assure the Americans that war is not likely to become cheaper, nor borrowing easier, as months pass on. The course of such things is very different. Each campaign opens new fields, absorbs new armies, and creates new charges. The great ball of debt, when once set rolling, will gather and grow till its dimensions outstrip all speculation. In our belief, the forcible subjugation of the South would prove a hopeless task, even if all the States of the North poured their wealth unsparingly into the Federal Exchequer, but if they attempt to defray its accumulating charges with money borrowed at 7 per cent., they will find themselves engaged in an expenditure which no country in the world could ever support.

And yet we went on for four years after this solemn warning, to which we showed a most unbecoming indifference, and borrowed money at 7 per cent. and actually at this time have the impudence to be living and prospering.

(From the *Saturday Review*, Dec. 7, 1861.)

It happens to be the unanimous opinion of ninteen educated Englishmen out of twenty that a more purposeless and hopeless enterprise than the reconquest of the South by the Federal Government has never been projected by any ancient or modern State.

This is the opinion. Farther on in the same article we find the following nice little reasons for that opinion.

If the war proceeds, it may perhaps become expedient to set right the errors or frauds of diplomacy by rectifying the boundary lines in Maine and in Oregon, and a superiority in arms will also be profitably employed in closing the vexatious dispute about San Juan; but, in general, England enters into the contest without a selfish impulse, for the purpose of coercing a rude and arrogant Government into the observance of national justice and courtesy. There will be little difficulty in applying the force which may be necessary for this purpose through the exclusive instrumentality of the fleet. No army will be required, except to assist in the defence of Canada: and the home garrisons can easily spare troops for this purpose without any serious augmentation of the peace establishment.

Oh! For further elucidation of the latter topic, read the anxious debates in Parliament and the articles in the London newspapers in the spring of 1864, on — the "Defence of Canada!"

The *Saturday Review* of February 8, 1862, having in the same number, with an entire absence of that national boastfulness which is so distinguishing a trait of the Yankees, said "Our position is so thoroughly superior to that of the Americans, that it is needless self-degradation" &c. &c., thus spoke *ex cathedra* upon the rebellion.

The illustration of general truths by contemporary experience is perfectly compatible with the absence of any desire to exult over the misfortunes and confusion of the *defunct Union*. The enterprise of the North was, from the first, seen to be *altogether hopeless*, but full allowance was made for the natural determination to try the fortune of war before final acquiescence in disruption. Only during the uncertainty arising from the *Trent* outrage was there any wish or expectation of taking a part in the quarrel, and there is now a general determination not to provide the Federalists with any pretext for excusing away their own *certain failure* by English interference. Sixty days will soon have passed away, and at the end of the term the South will not have been conquered, *and the resources of the Treasury will be exhausted.* When the experiment has been tried to the end, it will perhaps be thought that it is useless to recommence it.

Of course that settled the matter. One of the highest authorities of the nation which is "so thoroughly superior" having thus spoken, that was the end of the law. With a perversity entirely unaccountable however, in spite of this tremendous utterance, the matter would not stay settled.

(From the *Saturday Review* Feb. 8, 1862.)

That both England and the world at large have just now some heavy charges to bring against the Government and people of the United States is an assertion which we really need not stop to prove. That the civil war is a very unwise war, which cannot lead to any good object, is not the main point. That a war should seem useless and foolish to impartial spectators, while the belligerents enter into it heart and soul, is one of the commonest phenomena in the history of warfare. The North is just as foolish for trying to reconquer the South as we were eighty-five years ago for trying to reconquer North and South together. It is just as foolish as Englishmen were in those earlier times when they attached the idea of national glory and happiness to the conquest of France. It is just as foolish as Xerxes was when he led half the world against Athens, or as Napoleon was when he led half Europe against Russia. The mere folly is just as great and no greater, than in any of these cases.

Upon this theme as upon all others the presses of Richmond and those of London, with two distinguished exceptions — The *Daily News* and the *Spectator* — sung the same tune. But passing by the frothy outpourings at Richmond we may better listen to men high in office in the so called Confederacy. Even after the capture of New Orleans, the rebel Governor Moore thus held forth from Opelousas, June 18th, 1862.

THE STRUGGLE AND ITS SURE RESULT.

The loss of New Orleans, bitter humiliation as it was to Louisiana, has not created despondency, nor shaken our abiding faith in our success. Not to the expected eye of the enthusiastic patriot alone, who might be to color events with his hopes, but to the more impassioned gaze of the statesman, that success was certain from the beginning. . . Our recognition as a nation is one of those certainties of the future which nothing but our own unfaithfulness can prevent. We must not look around for friends for help when the enemy is straight before us. Help yourselves. It is the great instrument of national, as of individual success.

THOS. O. MOORE, Gov. of Louisiana.

OPELOUSAS, June 18, 1862.

The Northerners, though they have shown themselves more liable to delusion than any one could have believed of such a people, are not fools; and, in spite of the *boasting and lying of their Government,* [strange people, these Yankees, to be offended by language equally truthful and respectful,] they are receiving the conviction that such a people as the Confederates can never be subjugated. If it were a war for a fortress or a frontier, they would not be discouraged: but when they reflect on the object of the present invasion, and remember that they have undertaken not only to defeat the armies of Lee and Beauregard, but to utterly destroy them, to occupy the whole Southern territory [A task quite impossible!] and garrison it year after year with a standing army of at least a quarter of a million men, it may well be imagined that they are cooled and sobered by the prospect. We cannot but think that a great change of feeling is likely to take place at the North. The under currents of the popular mind are at first not visible; it is only when they have gained volume and strength that they can change the course of the stream. But there is enough to show that multitudes of the Northern people are becoming weary of this purposeless slaughter. About the temper of the business men there can be little doubt; they have been for many weeks giving to the cause of peace all the influence which their own timidity and the constitution of American society will allow them. But now we have fair grounds for believing that matters have gone further, and that the great body of the people are slowly coming round to the opinions of their less short-sighted countrymen. That these will be candid and confess their own madness is not to be expected. A people never recants. But they may show their rulers, by signs not to be mistaken, that they will tolerate, no more of Mr. Lincoln's crusade. The question will be soon determined. If this war is to go on, the immense levy ordered by the President must actually be made. The 300,000 men must be forthcoming if Virginia is to be held. *But they will not be forthcoming.* [This was in the year 1862.] We are told in the last dispatches that the volunteering makes slow progress, and the question of a conscription is still discussed. Our corespondent declares that in 11 days only 15,000 men had come forward, in spite of the enormous bounty, amounting in all to 150 dollars, that was offered to each man by the Federal and State Governments.

Draughting for service or in other words a conscription, was talked about: but we should think it would only be talked about. The scheme of a forcible levy of troops in a Republic to subjugate and hold down another Republic is one that will hardly be seriously proposed even by the more fanatical of Mr. Lincoln's advisers. All now, therefore, depends on the enlistment that is going on under the President's proclamation. If this fails, then all is over, and after a few months the independence of the South must be acknowledged, as it might have been with profit a twelve month ago.—*London Times*, July 26, 1862.

Not only the journalists but the statesmen of Great Britain announced to us our certain destruction, and in the kindness of their hearts bade us make our arrangements with that end in view. Mr. Roebuck, and even Mr. Gladstone, thus favored us in August 1862. Mr. Gladstone saying "Mr. Jefferson Davis has made of the South a nation" and that "separation is as certain as any event yet future and contingent."

(From *Mr. Roebuck's Sheffield Speech*.)

Touching upon the civil war in America, he [Mr. Roebuck] said he had at first looked at the disruption of the Union with grief, [In fact, though it is not generally known, Mr. Roebuck was drowned in sorrow.] but his present feeling was one of rejoicing. An irresponsible people, possessed of irresponsible and almost omnipotent power, was a people that could not be trusted; and he regarded the attempt of the North in endeavoring to restore the Union by force as an immoral proceeding totally incapable of success [Quite so Mr. Roebuck, without a doubt.] He therefore begged the noble lord deeply to consider whether the time had not come for him to be the first in Europe to ask the great Powers of Europe to recognize the Southern Confederacy. Six months would not pass over before that was done. [And they didn't pass, Mr. Roebuck; we all know they didn't.]

RECOGNITION OR MR. GLADSTONE'S REMOVAL.

(From the London *Morning Herald*, October 13, 1862.)

But, if immediate intervention be not desirable, there is no pretext for delaying the recognition of the Confederate States. That recognition jointly made by Russia, France and England, would be of service to the belligerents, and to mankind in general. It would withdraw from the North, in its wanton aggression upon the Confederates, that negative sanction which it has hitherto received from Europe. It would formally condemn further attempts to reconquer the South as hopeless, and therefore criminal. It would tend to strengthen the hands of the peace party at the North, and take away from their opponents the argument that, while foreign powers have not recognized the seceders, it is unreasonable to ask the Government which claims their allegiance to be the first to proclaim its own overthrow. To this recognition England — or rather the English Cabinet — is the sole obstacle. France is willing, and Russia will not refuse to follow the lead of France. And Sir John Parkinton has called attention to a system which ought to indicate an approaching change of policy on our part. When a Cabinet Minister distinctly and publicly declares that Mr. Davis has made of the South a nation, and that separation is as certain as any event yet future and contingent can be [as Mr. Gladstone did], he affirms that according to every recent rule and precedents the South is entitled to recognition.

We have seen what Governor Brown said after the taking of New Orleans; let us now see what that "great," "accomplished," "wise," and above all, that "prudent" and "reticent" statesman, Jefferson Davis, said, a few months before the fall of Vicksburg.

(*Speech before the Mississippi Legislature*, Dec. 26, 1862.)

I have confidence that Vicksburg will stand as before, and I hope that Johnston will find generals to support him if the enemy dare to land. Port Hudson is now strong. *Vicksburg will stand; and Port Hudson will stand;* but let every man that can be spared from other vocations, hasten to defend them, and thus hold the Mississippi river, that great artery of the Confederacy, preserve our communications with the trans-Mississippi department, and thwart the enemy's scheme of forcing navigation through to New Orleans. By holding that section of the river between Port Hudson and Vicksburgh, we shall secure these results, and the people of the West, cut off from New Orleans, will be driven to the East to seek a market for their products, and will be compelled to pay so much in the way of freights, that those products will be rendered almost valueless. Thus, I should not be surprised if the first daybreak of peace were to dawn upon us from that quarter. . . On my way here I stopped at the headquarters of Gen. Johnston. I knew his capacity and his resolution. I imparted to him my own thoughts, and asked him to come with me. I found that his ideas were directed in the same channel. He came in the shortest time for preparation, but whatever man can do will be done by him. I have perfect confidence that, with your assistance and support, he will drive the enemy from the soil of Mississippi.

There is some dispute as to the kind and the measure of punishment which should be inflicted upon Jefferson Davis. Would it be sufficient to commute the punishment to which he is liable by law to the reading to him, at intervals of a week or so, in his casemate at Fortress Monroe, all his speeches and " state papers " — those wonderfully " wise and sagacious " productions — from 1860 to 1865? To this there is however one insuperable objection,—" Cruel punishments " are forbidden by the Constitution.

THE FRENCH PEACE PROPOSITION.

We all remember that generous and purely disinterested offer of the French Government to mediate between the two confederate parties; and how Mr. Seward quietly replied that this government was quite able to manage its own affairs. But it may be interesting or at least amusing to refresh our memories of the manner in which that reply was received by the leading organs of British public opinion.

(From the *London Times*, Feb. 28, 1863.)

Either Mr. Seward can clearly discern what nobody else can distinguish, or he is without the power of seeing what is patent to the whole world besides. If he is not preternaturally right, he is incomprehensibly wrong. Taking his dispatches — as, of course, we must do for expressions of sincere and genuine convictions on the subject of the war — we find it almost impossible to imagine how opinions so unique could have been formed out of materials which are common to the whole world. Mr. Seward knows no more, or, at least, states no more, than is known to everybody in Europe as well as America, and yet, in the most decisive and peremptory tone, he announces conclusions which nobody in Europe, and, as we believe, few even in America, would think of accepting. . . . .

In this document he calmly, and even argumentatively, ignores every one of the lessons which Europe has involuntarily learnt from the events of the war. He, a Republican of 1863, depicts himself as no less incapable than an ancient Bourbon of learning anything at all. In his eyes there is no war between regular belligerents, but only an armed insurrection, which the United States are vigorously, and, as he maintains, triumphantly putting down. He denies that there are any two such parties, even, as North and South. He is not aware of any such distinction. . . .

After this, of course there was little room for the acceptance of the French proposals. Mr. Seward repudiates the idea of a Conference between a National Government and an insurgent force, precisely as he might have done before the first battle of Bull Run. He is much obliged to the French, but he will have none of it, and nothing, indeed, but misconceptions of fact, based on erroneous representations, could have suggested the proposition. That is the last phase of the American war as etched by Mr. Seward. We must allow that this picture of affairs is consistent — consistent, that is, with all that Mr. Seward has written from the beginning. It is the very story, without change or omission, which we have had, backed with his note of hand at "90 days' date," and renewed any number of times during the last two years. It is consistent enough, so far, beyond a doubt. Whether it has any consistency with facts or truth is a question which we had much rather leave to be decided by events than argue with Mr. Seward at present.

What a foolish person that Mr. Seward was; and how wise the *Times* editors; and how very small Mr. Seward must feel when he reflects how the *Times* poked fun at him and chaffed him, and gave him good and friendly advice! It was he who was incomprehensibly wrong, and the editor of the *Times* who was preternaturally right, to the tune of £10,000. The *Morning Post* (Ministerial organ) thus held forth upon this subject about this time:

"Perhaps Mr. Seward expects to gain in Washington, amongst certain classes, a little political capital, and, in exchange for that, is indifferent about the contempt he must incur in Europe. Still, emanating as this document does, from the Federal Cabinet, it is truly incredible that that body should have sunk so low as to indorse as its own, in the face of the world, so much arrant falsehood and absurd nonsense.

"Falsehood." Again we remark, what incomprehensible people the Yankees are to take offence at the tone of the British press.

At last came the victory of Gettysburg, and after it came these comments:

(From the *London Times*, July 21, 1863.)

We forecast very naturally and pleasantly, that as reunion is impossible, and the only object of fighting is to have the last blow, the winning side will be glad to make a kind and generous use of that vantage. Over and over again it has been hoped that the losing side might just retrieve its credit, in order to have something wherewith to enter on a Conference. Whether these hopes are founded on a just estimate of human nature or not, it is too evident that they were not founded on a just estimate of American nature. There must be other influences at work beyond the hope of final success, which is impossible, or of an amicable compromise, or of any other national result. . . . . Whether the Federals are ever beaten into peace or not, it is evident they will never be softened into kindness by success. The least advantage, however dearly purchased, and be it ever so trifling in the great balance of war, brings them to the balcony, and sends them to "the God of Battles" and "the eternal justice of their cause." When this is all that victory, all that religion teaches them, we reasonably ask when will they ever condescend to be reasonable and wise. The awful sanctions and sacred examples which they abuse might tell them another lesson. There is in the very manner of this obstinacy so much mere exultation that we must conclude the spirit of the Federal cause to be the chief obstacle to peace.

What a generous and sagacious view is here! A people sacrifice the flower of their young men by tens of thousands; they spend, each man contributing from his own hard earnings, millions a day for years; hardly a family in the land in which there is not one dead or exposed to death; (what is the hope of saving £10,000 or of getting £15,000, without paying a shilling, to this?) and yet the only object is "to have the last blow." And that extraordinary conclusion, so true in one sense, so wide from the truth in the sense intended,— that the chief obstacle to peace is "the spirit of the Federal cause."

THE SAME OLD STORY.

(From the *London Times*, July 12, 1864.)

This is the fourth year of the war, and also the fourth and last year of Mr. Lincoln Presidentship. He entered on office in March, 1861, but his election in the previous November led to the secession of many of the Southern States before the close of the year. Practically, therefore, in respect to the influence which it exercised, his tenure of office may be regarded as having commenced four months before he took up his residence at the White House, and will in like manner terminate as soon as his successor is appointed. We do not think, therefore, that the present Administration will have the opportunity, even if it possessed the inclination or the means, of projecting another invasion of Virginia on a scale similar to the recent one. But will their successors pursue the policy which has hitherto so signally failed, or will the population of the Northern States elect a Chief Magistrate who will follow in the footsteps of Mr. Lincoln? We are inclined to think not. We will not now reiterate the arguments which, from the commencement of the civil war, have satisfied every unprejudiced mind of the futility of the enterprise undertaken by the Northern Republic, and which each succeeding month has served to corroborate. The war is now, as we stated, in its fourth year, and what progress have the Northern States made toward the completion of their work of conquest? In the Border State of Virginia their armies have never, during the entire war, gained a single victory. [True, Antietam and Gettysburg were not won within the limits, although they were won against the army of Virginia. But Malvern Hill, from which the rebel forces fled according to their own accounts " amid the cheers of the Union troops " was won in Virginia; and after it a general with the aggressive spirit of a cock sparrow would have marched straight into Richmond.] This is a fact which, taking into consideration the numerous occasions on which the rival armies came in collision, and the many vicissitudes of warfare, is very remarkable. Everywhere — at New-Orleans, on the Mississippi, and in Tennesee — the armies of the Northern Confederacy gained what in appearance were substantial victories, but which have not, even in the slightest degree, tended to bring the Southern States under the control of the original Government.

It is impossible to believe that the population of the Northern States do not perceive that which is patent to the eyes of every one on this side of the Atlantic, and it is difficult to suppose that they will much longer continue on the road to ruin. Everything will turn upon the expression of public opinion, as manifested at the approaching Presidential election. There are many who will still maintain the expediency of continuing to prosecute the war, and will demand the reëstablishment of the Union. But they are not the majority of the population. Those who have accumulated wealth through the factitious impetus which the war gives to trade, the " shoddy " aristocracy of the Northern cities, will be loud in their demands for the subjugation of the South; and those who hope to become wealthy before the crash which will follow the suspension of hostilities will echo this cry. But the more far-sighted, who know that to continue the war is only to add to the immense debt already created, and so increase the evils which will unquestionably sooner or later fall as a punishment on the people of the Northern States for having wasted their resources, will as earnestly require that those to whom the direction of public affairs shall be intrusted shall seek by every means in their power to bring the war to a speedy end. Already preparations are being made for the election of Mr. Lincoln's successor, and it is in connection with that election that the discomfiture of the grand army of the North will possess its chief importance.

AGAIN.

(From the London *Times* of October 10, 1864.)

We see the frantic patient tearing the bandages from his wounds and thrusting aside the hand that would assuage his miseries, and every day that the war goes on we see less and less probability that the great fabric of the Union will ever be reconstructed in its original form, and more and more likelihood that the process of disintegration will extend far beyond the present division between North and South. We observe the rapid destruction of that mighty fabric of prosperity which was so formidable a rival to our own colonies, and we look forward, at no distant date, to the day when the credit of the Republic must be hopelessly and utterly destroyed. Were we really animated by the spirit of hostility which is always assumed to prevail among us towards America, we should view the terrible spectacle with exultation and delight, we should rejoice that the American people, untaught by past misfortunes, have resolved to continue the war to the end, and hail the probable continuance of the power of Mr. Lincoln as the event most calculated to pledge the nation to a steady continuance in its suicidal policy. But we are persuaded that the people of this country view the prospect of another four years of war in America with very different feelings. They are not able to divest themselves of sympathy for a people of their own blood and language [" the scum of the earth," — ROEBUCK ; " a nuisance among the nations," — *Morning Herald*; " barbarians," " blackguards."— *Saturday Review*.] thus wilfully rushing down the path that leadeth to destruction.

* * * * * * *

Ruin stares the Union in the face if the war is to be conducted by General M'Clellan, and if it be conducted by President Lincoln the result must be exactly the same. Why should we feel anxiety as to the success of one party or the other, when either must be equally fatal to the welfare of the Republic and equally pernicious to the cause of liberty and good Government throughout the world ?

SAD FOREBODINGS

(From the London *Times* of Dec. 22d, 1864.)

Last and dreariest of all are the President's views on the prospects of peace. No negotiation can do any good. The Union must be preserved. The South insists on severing it. The President recommends, by way of a peace-offering, the total abolition of slavery — a measure sure to be passed sooner or later, and which, he thinks, may as well be done at once. " It is still open to " all to lay down their arms and seek pardon, but " the time may come, probably will come, when " public duty shall demand that the avenue to " grace shall be closed." Thus, without apparently possessing any confidence that he can bring the war to a speedy or successful termination, does the President refuse all reconciliation, except on terms which he well knows the Southern leaders cannot and will not acccept, — the laying down their arms, suing for pardon, immediate abolition of slavery, and restoration of the Union as it was four years ago. The vessel is driving straight on the rocks, and the helmsman will not move his hand to the right or to the left in order to avoid a collision which must shatter it to atoms.

Poor foolish helmsman! If he had only hearkened to the British Bunsby who can give "an opinion as is an opinion," he would not have seen his rickety craft wrecked, ruined, shattered to atoms.

And here we have our own dear Morning *Herald* again, the mouth-piece of the collective wisdom of the Carleton club:

(From the *Morning Herald*, March 4, 1865.)

Look at the Americans now, at the date of their grand political celebration, and what do we behold? Not even the solemnity of a civil war. Only fury, levity and an atrocious disregard of nature: only a charlatanism which has ceased to dazzle: only riot, destruction, and brutality. There is a legend extant which tells how the First Napoleon, in a dream invented for him by some artistic poet, felt wounded in his heart when he reviewed his dead legions in the Elysian fields of Paris; but the pang his conscience felt must have been as nothing compared with the sting to Abraham Lincoln, were it credible that the representative rail-splitter ever had a conscience at all. . . A civil war, of horrible ferocity, spreads itself like a deadly exhalation over the land, and there is not a single American statesman in office competent or willing to guide his nation out of the disastrous abyss. America, as an American orator ejaculated once, is "England without a past!" This fourth day of March disposes us to ask her politicians upon what calculations they base their calculation of chances for the future. They can have no pride in their present position; they can have little hope; they have seen their constitution wrecked, and where are they at this hour? In a word, what are we expecting from day to day, from their vast and teeming continent? Intelligence of war, of carnage, of misery, and social degradation, over which a people, celebrating a disgraced anniversary, must blush and be bitterly ashamed.

We do blush; we are ashamed. We put our hands upon our mouths and our mouths in the dust, and we bow down before our elder brother the great, the wise John Bull.

BLUNDER UPON BLUNDER.

The war went on, and in the Spring of the present year the prospect was not exactly that which had been seen through the spectacles of the London *Times*. Whereupon there began to be a dreadful twitter in the governing classes of Great Britain — a fearful looking for of judgment to come, and upon this the *Times* worked, hoping, according to all appearances, to keep up animosity and to run with the current of opinion which it sought to control. Whereupon Mr. Forster, M. P. for Bradford, accused the *Times* in the House of asserting that "there could be no question but that the Federals would go to war with us whenever a prospect of success presented itself." This was in a debate upon the Canadian defences. Whereupon the *Times* replied and read Mr. Forster this little lecture:

> We have left ourselves but little room for our own case with these gentlemen. Mr. Forster, we are sorry to tell so amiable a gentleman, has committed a double inaccuracy. He charges us with asserting positively that, upon the restoration of peace, Federals and Confederates will join to invade Canada, and with wishing that the war may last. We neither made the assertion nor expressed the wish. . . . . We do not assert, and never have asserted, that the two belligerents will unite to invade Canada.

Whereupon certain uncomfortable persons quoted the following passage from a *Times* leading article.

(From the London *Times*, March 8, 1865.

> As the Federal Government maintains that it has a quarrel with us in the shape of claims which we do not acknowledge, and it has a great deal to gain by successful war with us, the question to which we have to address ourselves is simply *whether they can go to war with us with a fair prospect of success. If they can they certainly will.*

Whereupon the *Times* said nothing.

The events of the spring of 1865 took place. Sherman succeeded in reaching the sea-board with " all of his army that he could save," and thereupon the *Times* trumpet began to give an uncertain sound, which a certain sturdy, steady voice from Manchester proclaimed. Whereupon came this shuffling answer.

Mr. Bright tells us that the English Press was mistaken on American affairs and is trying to back out of its mistakes. We admit that we have been mistaken about American affairs, but it has been in a sense exactly the contrary to that which he imputes to us. We certainly have greatly under-estimated the resources, the courage, and the tenacity of the South. When the war began we did not expect the South would be able to offer so determined a resistance to its opponents: we thought that the immense forces which the North was able to bring into the field must necessarily break through the weaker line of their opponents. ["Hear, hear" from a gentleman who has lost his memory, and groans from some gentlemen who lost their money.] We could not anticipate — and we are not ashamed of having been deceived — the long series of bloody battles which have compelled such a succession of Northern Generals and armies to yield to the prowess of a weak and despised enemy. We thought that the Southern line would have been speedily broken through: that the principal cities of the Confederacy would probably fall into the hands of the invaders, and that Northern armies would have been able to traverse almost at will the territories which supply the materials of rebellion. These things are now beginning to come to pass, only they have come to pass much later and in a much less degree than we had anticipated: but then we thought and still think, that the real dangers and difficulties of the contest will begin. These territories are too vast to be occupied, and the elements of rebellion they contain are too rife to be left to themselves. They may be penetrated in every direction, but we do not see how they are to be held or subdued. It remains to be seen whether we are wrong in these anticipations.

Well, it has been seen. What a laugh of scorn this passage must have provoked from honest John Bright!

THE MONEY QUESTION.

Upon no subject is our cousin John more oracular than that of finance. When he speaks upon finance he summons the world to listen to the words of wisdom. *He* understands this thing; other people don't. But of all the ignorant simpletons in the matter of money management, John knows none so ignorant and so foolish as Jonathan. That isn't the worst of it; he is a thieving scoundrel. Borrows your money and buys your goods, and then says, not that he can't pay but that he won't pay, that he don't owe you anything,—repudiates, in fact. Then having told Jonathan this, he wonders what the fellow finds to take offence at, and why he won't listen to good, friendly disinterested advise. Perhaps this was John's strongest point during the war. He began to hold forth upon it early and he continued his outpourings even until the end. He was instant in season and out of season. He gave us precept upon precept and precept upon precept, here a little and there a great deal; and he bid largely for our good will by telling the world and us that if we borrowed any money we should be sure to refuse to pay it; that our war debt would be repudiated as surely as it was incurred That we had paid our only war debt, principle and interest in a few years when we were only 8,000,000 of people, and that no creditor of this Republic ever lost a dollar justly due him, or failed to receive it on the day when it was due, and that on the contrary President Jackson was obliged to say to France and Spain, "pay up this debt you have been shirking so long instantly, or fight," and then they paid,— that these were the facts was of course of no consequence whatever. John had decided that Jonathan was "utterly ignorant of the first principles of political economy" and also that he was a "d—d repudiating scoundrel," and that is the end of the law. Therefore did the *Times* and the *Saturday Review*, the two wisest and most influential organs of British public opinion, predict sudden financial ruin for the United States, and continue their prophesyings, mingled with denunciation, for four years, announcing weekly, during that period, the speedy coming of the financial crash which never came.

The *Saturday Review* thus led off.

(From the *Saturday Review*, June 15, 1861.)

There are still stronger reasons against a war on a great scale, inasmuch as it can only be carried on with a great standing army. It is easier to bluster about half a million of men than to feed and pay 100,000. The people of the United States are little accustomed to taxes, nor will it be easy to incur a large debt which would be repudiated as soon as it became necessary to provide for the interest. If the sacrifice were undergone, the Republic would have provided itself with a master, in the form of an alien body of veteran mercenaries. The rank and file of the regular army will be Irish, with, perhaps, an admixture of Germans; and, as Americans are well aware, no race is either braver or more indifferent to constitutional forms.

But great as the losses may be to the invester in prairie consols or Arkansas tooth-picks, it will be nothing to the fate that awaits him who dabbles either in Federal or State stocks contracted for war purposes. His money will be as inevitably lost as if it were sunk in the Suez canal or the Atlantic cable. [What is the present opinion of Sir Henry de Houghton, Mr. Beresford Hope, Mr. John Laird, Mr. John T. Delane and others their fellow bondholders upon this subject?] Spasmodic efforts will doubtlessly be made to pay the interest of such loans during the continuance of the war; but the result is assured, and may be summed up in one word — repudiation.—*Ibid.*

The Liverpool *Courier* of August 7th, in the same year thus followed suit.

Now the Federal Government have determined to levy a *regular* army of 150,000 men. How long will it take to discipline such a host as that with the means at the disposal of the Cabinet?' Where will money be procured, for no European capitalists were inclined to lend even at 7 per cent. to a confederacy which has once legalised "repudiation." [What do they call it in Liverpool when a man deliberately tells the thing that is not, for the purpose of injuring his neighbor?] If before defeat it was difficult to procure a loan of £80,000,000, after defeat it becomes impossible. Add to this the loss of heart, the loss of prestige, the doubt and hesitation, consequent on such a failure. If at last a regular army of 150,000 should be enrolled, we may well ask, how long would the Northern states constitute a republic? [Not a day, sir, not a day!]

Whatever may have been thought before, it is now plain that he Southerners can resist, and that the war will be protracted. There is an end to Mr. Bright's dream of a quick solution of the difficulty. The Southerners would now accept nothing less than a full acknowledgment of their independence and of their right to secede. The war may be carried on for years, but this must be the result at last.

Of one thing John Bull was sure, that we would not submit to taxation by "the central government." To pay any thing was foreign to our habits; to pay taxes, although for the discharge of our honest debts, something not to be thought of.

(From the *Saturday Review* of August 10th, 1861.)

It has now become certain that Secession cannot be trampled out on the instant; and *it was always certain that the Northern States would never be able to conquer the South in a balanced and prolonged war.*

There will be more difficulty in raising money than enlisting recruits; . . . . . and there is reason to hope that the London money market will be inaccessible to borrowers *who would inevitably repudiate the obligation,* while they would probably *contrive a war as a pretext for their refusal to pay.*

What an incomprehensible people these Yankees are, that they don't like, — in fact, actually resent, the reiterated assertion, not that there are dishonest men among them, as there are among all people, but that they are a nation of rogues and scoundrels! — murderers, too, who will deliberately get up a fight and kill their creditors by the thousand, to rid themselves of the necessity of paying their honest debts! What wonder that the *Saturday Review,* of all papers, should express its surprise at "the bitter feeling against Great Britain in" — sweet phrase! —"Federal America!"

(From the London *Times*, June 24, 1862.)

"We had and, besides, have still the very gravest doubts as to the ability of the Central Government to enforce upon so many almost independent States the payment of a heavy amount of taxes. We thought we saw reason for believing that the West, poor and warlike, would think it had done enough in breaking the long line of the Confederates, and would refuse to bear its share in the heavy general burden, and we are confirmed in this view by remembering how very light is the taxation to which America has hitherto submitted, and how totally new and unprecedented is the notion of the payment of a direct tax to the Central Government."

So decided the London oracle; and yet the people here most perversely and absurdly insisted upon being taxed, clamored because Congress held back from taxation, and yielded cheerfully to a system of taxation that entered their very households, and soon drew from them nearly a million of dollars a day. A most contrary people! never will do as they are desired!

(From the London *Times*, January 31, 1863.)

The Americans are doing their best to amuse and instruct the world. [But it so happens that neither the amusement nor the instruction were all on one side.] We have no need of amphitheatres of gladiators, of wild beasts, of burning Christians, and all the other amusements of the jaded old Roman; for we cannot unfold a paper without the description of some desperate conflict between all the varied means of human destruction. We ought to be obliged to people who undertake at such a sacrifice to relieve the tedium of civilized existence.

This is the respectful and considerate way in which the leading journal of the British empire speaks of a war which was deciding the fate of a great Republic, and the freedom of a race, and to which a people of its own blood and language was giving the flower of its manhood and the sum total of its wealth! And the Yankees don't like it! Singular people!

The Americans have taken a plunge into the infinite. They are breasting the waves of the Atlantic in the very maddest attempt that ever wearied madman. They have infinite territory, infinite people, infinite water power, infinite corn and cotton, infinite destiny, infinite brag; the other day they broached an infinite reservoir of oil, they have now tapped infinite credit. They feel as the youth does with a constitution, a fortune, a character — everything whole and untouched. He can never get to the end of them; at least it is a very long time yet. Bystanders know better. We, too, know better how it is faring with the Americans — with the Federals even more than the Confederates, inasmuch as the former trust most to money, the latter to men. .... Thus far, we are assured by the Federal financiers that things go on wonderfully as usual, and out of the very range of the war it could not be guessed that the country was being drained of its men and money, that the armies had been decimated and the soil ravaged. This may continue long, except that deaths and wounds, reaching up to this time to about a quarter of a million in the aggregate of both sides, must tell very seriously on the general wealth and prosperity. But any body whose property consists in paper money or in fixed interest, such as that of the state debt or guaranteed dividends, must suffer very great loss and be reduced to utter poverty. The material resources of the country will remain not only untouched, but in many cases relieved by the diminution of fixed outgoings. Land, its produce, houses, mines, ships, and, above all, the strong arm and the active mind, will be worth as much as ever, till the catastrophe comes to such a pass as to discourage enterprise, destroy confidence, and so far dissolve society itself, weaken its power of mutual aid, and place its prizes beyond certain calculation or reasonable hope. *These miseries and worse are before America; for the destruction of mutual confidence means much worse than can be conceived by any American in his present crazy mood.* Every rise in the premium of gold, slight and unobtrusive as the little figure or fraction may seem, is a step in the downward direction — *to what depth is probably past all expression, calculation, or conception.*

The extracts from the London *Times* thus far given in this volume are chiefly taken from leading articles in that paper, the editor in chief of which is shown by recent revelations to have been pecuniarily interested, to the amount of £10,000. in the downfall of the Republic upon whose affairs he set himself before the British public as a fair and honorable adviser. But hardly less important than its leading articles are the well known City articles of that paper, which for several years past have been written by Mr. M. B. Sampson, who was similarly interested, as the same records show, to the amount of £15,000 in Confederate bonds, *for which he was to pay nothing.* Under these very peculiar circumstances, what views he presented of affairs in this country will appear by the following and subsequent extracts from his articles.

SOME CHEERFUL PREDICTIONS.

(From the *London Times*, City Article, August 28, 1864.)

The premium on gold in New York has again declined, the last quotation being 25.5. The confidence of the people in the financial manipulations of Mr. Chase can be compared only to that which in this country was concentrated upon Mr. Hudson during the railway mania.

* * * * * * *

So long as the expenditure of the country is in excess of its annual production, the march in this direction is inevitable. Nothing can avert it, although many circumstances may delay it, and there can be no question that Mr. Chase has shown singular adroitness in the latter process. Of course, to any persons financial experience, even at New York, the end must be perfectly plain; [Certainly, of course, manifestly, without a doubt, inevitably, can't be otherwise, because don't you see, and ah—ah—all that sort of thing?] but Mr. Chase has stifled the warning that these persons would by their operations otherwise give, by causing a prohibition to be enacted against buying or selling gold for delivery at a future date. In London there are many merchants who would at once order their New-York agents to commence operations of this description if the freedom which all other cities enjoy existed in that quarter. But, such not being the case, there is nothing that can cause the market to take its natural course so long as the Government can procure enough gold for the remittance hither by each steamer. The diminution in our demand for grain this year will greatly accelerate the final collapse, but if the people can be kept from panic there may still be several months of happy infatuation. [That was cheering; and even now to look back upon it is encouraging.] If it were possible to ascertain the amount of specie that existed in the country at the commencement of the drain, the period of dis-illusion might be fixed with almost mathematical precision [Why "almost?" Why this unbecoming modesty? Why not with mathematical precision, to a minute?] This being impossible, all that the commercial world can do is to wait and watch. One thing is important to be remembered,—namely, that all the triumphs the North may gain can but make its financial affairs worse. With a peace founded on an agreement for separation, the accounts for the past might be made up, and a definitively reduced expenditure might be adopted for the future. With the South to be held by force of armies, a subjugated province, all hope of a return to economy must forever be abandoned.

ANOTHER OPINION.

(From the London *Times*, City Article, July 13, 1864.)

"A partial rally in United States bonds occurred yesterday and some large amounts were again taken for the Continent. The recovery was consequent on the reported resignation of Mr. Chase, the Secretary of the Treasury. Looking at the point to which he has brought the Federal finances, it is only natural that a rumor of his retirement should create an improved feeling, but whoever may be his successor, only one course is open to arrest the present ruin, and there seems as little prospect as at any former time of its being adopted. A cessation of the war is the sole condition on which then the faintest hopes of anything short of an utter financial breakdown can be based. Unless Mr. Lincoln means peace, there is no use in his changing his Finance Minister. For providing the means for the expenditure of £200,000,000 a year, no one could excel Mr. Chase, who has adroitly contrived to get as large a proportion from it as possible from foreign admirers.

Well, Mr. Lincoln did not mean peace; and yet within less than one year from the publication of this article United States bonds were worth more in London than they were in New York. But there was "a cessation of hostilities." Certainly, they ceased very manifestly and decidedly one day last April; and peace ensued; and as this was Mr. Lincoln's purpose, he did "mean peace" all the time; and so the *Times*' city article was sensible and sound, and a good guide to the British capitalist after all. As good as the oracle which said "*Aio te Romanos vincere posse.*" Truly if we could have been slain by the jaw bone of an ass, this Samson would have put an end to us.

We began upon this topic with an extract from the *Saturday Review* of June 1861; we shall conclude with one from the same candid and courteous paper published February 8th, 1865, nearly four years afterward. Some worthies are never weary in well doing.

THE FINANCES OF THE UNITED STATES.

(From the *Saturday Review*, February 8, 1865.)

Perhaps the most striking circumstances in recent accounts from America is the great coolness with which the people of the North contemplate the insolvency of their Government. They know that the old boast about patriotic loans of indefinite extent has collapsed before enough had been raised in this shape to meet a single quarter's expenditure. [The rogue means that this should be taken as evidence of his sagacity; but we know that he had secret information from Mr. Chase, and Mr. Fessenden, and Mr. McCulloch.] They know too, probably better than we do, that the often-repeated assurance that taxes shall be imposed sufficient at least to cover the interest on the debt will never be realized. Like its promises to pay, the promises to tax of the Federal Government will be redeemed in paper. [Plainly this knowledge was also derived from the bureau of Internal Revenue at Washington; the receipts of which at the time when this article was written were only about $1,000,000 a day.] An abstract resolution in favor of raising by taxation a revenue of not less than 30,000,000*l.* has been almost unanimously voted by Congress, but among the financial arrangements which are said to have met with favor, there is included a condition that direct taxation shall be postponed as long as possible. That it is unconstitutional, if not illegal, is the smallest of the objections to it. The real difficulty is that an income-tax would not be paid, [*Never!* NEVER!! NEVER!!!] and unless half of the 600,000 men of the Federal army are to be employed, like Austrian soldiers, in collecting taxes, all the votes that can be passed may fail to extract the longed for dollars from Western farmers, or even from the traders of the Atlantic seaboard. [Certainly; the few straggling dollars that are obtained, we all know to our sorrow, are extorted at the point of the bayonet by hireling soldiers who accompany the tax-gatherers.] In a country like the United States, it is one thing to vote a revenue, and another to levy it. Voluntary loans and taxes are indeed admitted on all hands to be incapable of supplying the requirements of the war, and yet we find the commercial journals of New York discussing the financial crisis more cheerfully than we should speak of a deficit of two or three millions. . . . . Once for all, the capital of the country may thus be made to produce the means of providing the army for a month or two, and then there will be an end of the resource. [What a prophet! Where is Daniel's glory now?] . . . . . It is very difficult to believe — in spite of the tall talk about the Union — that financial difficulties on so enormous a scale will not put a speedy end to the aimless crusade of the Northern States. [Alas! it is ended.]

MILITARY MATTERS.

The other of the two points upon which John Bull was strongest, was of course the military aspect of the war. The opinions which he delivered upon finance we have already had an opportunity of re-examining under the light of recent events. A perusal of the following passages, extracted chiefly from the great British authority upon all subjects, will show that he was no less sagacious and penetrating in his judgment upon military events than he was upon the less striking, but hardly less important, movements by which our Treasury provided supplies for the War Office.

THE MILITARY PROSPECT OF THE GOVERNMENT

(From the London *Times*, September, 1861.)

Were England at this moment to announce to the world its intention to make the speediest possible conquest of France, or were France to make the same declaration as to England, the world would laugh at the egregious folly that had inspired the design and prompted the boast. The world would grant that, supposing either people to be infatuated enough, and obstinate enough, it could inflict enormous and irreparable injuries on the other, but only at the cost of equal injuries to itself. . . . . Now, that is the case of the two Confederacies across the Atlantic, where the surviving half of an effete Federal Union has undertaken to reduce the other half to its Federal duties. We say that this is the case, but before we proceed a step further, it is neccessary to observe that the case of the Northern Americans is in some important respects more difficult than ours would be. They have to protect more than a thousand miles of land frontier, including one closely beleagured position surrounded by foes or ill-affected adherents. Speaking the same language as their foe, they have no means of excluding spies from their lines, or even traitors from their ranks. [True.] They have to make a standing army and a fleet. [True, and we did it, John.] They have to learn the first elements of tactics, and even military discipline. [But you forget the invaluable lessons we received by every steamer.] They are without soldiers, or officers to command and to train them. [Lamentable destitution, wasn't it, John?]

Lastly, war, which changes its character according to circumstances, establishes special rules of probability for different localities. The one rule established by all American warfare is that the advantage is on the side of the defence. Our offensive operations always failed against fortified positions, against breastworks thrown up in a night, against forests full of an invisible foe ; against heat, hunger and thirst ; against the ever imminent flank attack ; against the certainty that every step diminished the number, the strength and the munitions of our own men, and increased those of the enemy. [Therefore, of course the Yankees must fail; and so they did John, so they did.] The present war might, for its incidents, be a chapter in our own disastrous wars on that soil.

There is only one enterprise which can be compared to this, and is the First Napoleon's gigantic, but infatuated attempt upon Russia. If any one will attempt to compare the means of the Federalists with those of Napoleon, he will find them far inferior in every respect; while there is no doubt that the Southern States are far more able to defend every point, every position, every line in their territory, than the Russians were in theirs. [Good boy ! What is your present conclusion from those premises?] They have mountainous ranges instead of steppes ; they have a population accustomed to carry arms, and only too glad to use them ; they have railways, and abundance of food and other necessaries of war. They are evidently superior in generalship, and in the social organization best adapted for war. [Quite invincible, you see ! A nation of Spartans led by Mars himself !]

We are in a condition to offer advice. [Singular condition for you to be in, John. Never was heard of before.] We can advise the Northern States of America, as we can advise the legitimate Princes and the despotic Courts of Europe. Let the statesmen at Washington only do what England has done before a hundred times, and what all Europe has done, is doing, and will still do. Let the Northern States "accept the situation," as we did eighty years ago upon their own soil; as Austria did two years ago at Villafranca and Zurich. Let them count the cost before they march forth to drive half a million armed men a thousand miles across their own country into the Gulf of Mexico. Let them consider whether they can do what Napoleon could not do in the plentitude of his power, with many times their number, their stores, their credit, and above all, their military skill and experience, his school of Generals, and his supply of veterans. What they propose to do and be is not only to be as good as the Southerners, or a little the better, but overwhelmingly superior. Are they ? Is not this an overweening opinion of themselves ? Can they drive the Southerners like a flock of sheep, smoke them out of their own nests like wasps, ferret them like rabbits, and bag them like game? Of course not. [Ask General Lee, and General Johnston, and General Kirby Smith.]

AFTER THE BATTLE OF CHANCELLORSVILLE.

(From the London *Times*, May 19, 1863.)

The only chance of his success seemed to be that Sedgwick should be able to operate on Lee's right flank and rear before Hooker was crushed. We can anticipate no more hopeful tidings from the Government at Washington having kept back the news of the result of Monday's battle. If it should have been unfavorable, we do not wonder at their hesitating to proclaim so great a calamity. *If Gen. Hooker is defeated, the last chance of success, at least in Virginia, is gone.* The only General who has shown any enterprise or activity will have been hopelessly beaten. It is clear from the accounts of the battle that the German corps had entered solely for the sake of the bounty money, and were not to be depended upon even in the first attack. What would be the chance of raising a new Army of the Potomac with the only remaining General beaten, his troops demoralized, none but foreigners willing to volunteer, and those worthless at the first assault?

There's a situation for you! The last chance in Virginia gone, the only remaining General beaten, none but foreigners willing to volunteer, and those worthless! And yet these perverse Yankees actually had the impudence to find one more general named Meade, and afterwards another named Grant, nay, three besides, named Sherman and Sheridan and Thomas, and to volunteer themselves, and actually to succeed even in Virginia when they had not a chance. Incomprehensible and insufferable people, those Yankees! Really "a nuisance among the nations;" especially to people who had £10,000, £15,000, £50,000, or from that to £180,000 dependent on their failure.

(From the London *Times*, May 25, 1863.)

What was the Army of the Potomac good for if it was to sit interminably on the north side of the Rappahanock, without so much as attempting the invasion of Virginia and capture of Richmond for which it had been raised? An answer to this question had been given by General McClellan who told his countrymen in plain words that the march to Richmond was impracticable, in as much as the Confederates were masters of the country, and able to defend position after position against any force of invaders. The Federals possessed no army strong enough to cut their way to the Confederate capital through such troops as would oppose their passage. This was plain sense but it was not very palatable. It involved something like a confession that the South could not be conquered and that the war was hopeless, for how were the Confederate States to be subdued if the single State of Virginia could not be recovered..... [Of course it was impossible to subdue the rest first and Virginia last.] What McClellan thought must happen to any army attempting the enterprise, has actually happened to the army of the Potomac. What Hooker said could be done he found it impossible to do. He discovered that the enemy of whom he had spoken so lightly was in reality stronger than himself, able to disconcert his plans, check his advance and drive him back headlong to his quarters. This is precisely what other commanders had predicted, but what Hooker had refused to believe. He is now probably less incredulous, but will the Government and people of the North have their eyes opened to the truth? *They cannot take Richmond.* They have made the trial, with a succession of armies under a succession of Generals and from a variety of points. They have tried caution and audacity, strategy and recklessness in turn, and they have failed in every effort alike. The result teaches Europe no more than it knew before, but if it should impart a conviction to the Federals that they are indeed engaged in a work beyond their strength, it may conduce to a termination of this hopeless war.

The similarity of the style in which the Richmond and the London newspapers spoke of the military movements against the rebellion is very remarkable. If we did not know that the following passage, announcing the beginning of Grant's movement upon Richmond, was from the *Richmond Examiner*, we might be in doubt whether it was from the London *Times*, the *Saturday Review*, or the London *Morning Herald*.

GRANT'S COMBINATIONS RIDICULED.

(From the *Richmond Examiner*, March 30, 1864.)

Amongst other intelligence conveyed to the Yankee papers by their Washington correspondents, we find this:
. "Agents of the Sanitary Commission at the front have for the past few days, been making requisitions for stimulants, &c. on their principal officer here." When there is a great demand for stimulants for the Army of the Potomac, we may always know that it is expected to fight soon. That army has consumed more whiskey than ammunition since May last; and, indeed, our men can always snuff an approaching assault, if the men happen to be

to windward, by the odor of old rye tainting the breeze. They are not for the future to rely upon this indication with implicit confidence: because it is said that one main element of Grant's confidence this time is, that he is always to wait until the wind shifts; that as deer-stalkers keep to leeward of their game, so Grant expects to stalk the Army of Northern Virginia.

In the meantime Thomas and Stoneman may have adventures before they join hands with Sheridan; and as to Sherman, he has "taken to digging." [Poor Sherman!] It seems to be his fundamental maxim that he is not to fight; and we have seen that the moment he is attacked he begins intrenching. At that game his progress northward, in the face of so wary an indefatigable an opponent as Johnston, is likely to be slow: it will scarcely be sufficiently advanced within those "ten days" which Grant allowed Richmond to surrender. Such, however, is the combination which we have now to face and to baffle, and to do it within a month. If it break down anywhere, as there is very good hope, then the peril for this year will be over; and it will be for Lincoln and Seward to consider a new plan for approaching Richmond, and also to invent a new, great General to carry into effect. For both Grant and Sherman must then be shelved: their ideas of conducting a siege will be pronounced not wide and grand enough for the Yankee nation. Their combinations were not extensive enough — their several approaches did not converge from sufficiently distant points. Next year the siege of Richmond must be commenced by opening trenches at Key West in Florida, and Corpus Christi in Texas, and digging through the continent so as to meet and co-operate with another advance commencing from the upper waters of the Arkansas River. [What scathing irony! But whom does it scathe?]

GRANT'S FAILURE AND THE END OF ALL THINGS.

(From the *Morning Herald*, May 13, 1864.)

We know almost enough of the campaign in Virginia to declare Grant's advance upon Richmond a failure, and to express a confident hope that the last fiery trial of the Southern Confederacy has been safely passed.

From other parts of the Southern States the news is scarcely less cheering to the Confederates. The advance upon Atlanta is a failure. [Utter.] Johnston's position is said to be too strong for attack. [That's the reason he left it.] We shall probably learn in a few days that here also the attack has been made and repulsed. From the Red River the news continues most disastrous to the Federal arms, and gold in New York is at 75 premium. How will the New York mob submit to the draft. And where are the soldiers to enforce it? [Nowhere. And that point is settled.]

GRANT A FAILURE. RICHMOND CAN'T BE TAKEN.

(From the *London Times*, August 22, 1864.)

To the war in Virginia the Federals devoted their best army, their main stores of material, and their most determined Commander. The force which advanced southwards at the beginning of May was the strongest force ever equipped by the North, and it was in excellent hands. If Grant was not an accomplished General, he was an intrepid and resolute soldier, proof against discouragement, and bent upon winning at all hazards and by any means. Nevertheless up to this hour he has been completely foiled by the superior skill of his antagonists; and the resources at his command are now to all appearance so nearly exhausted that it is hard to see what success greater than a safe retreat remains within his reach. He has kept his promise of "fighting it out all the summer," but without the result which he anticipated. Through three long months he has marched and countermarched, manœuvred and fought, until no new device or strategy seems left to be tried, but the end is that Richmond is safe while Washington is menaced, and that Lee is master of the field. It is true that the campaign is not yet over, and that war is full of uncertainties; but the strongest partisans of the Federal cause can hardly expect that the Virginian expedition will be anything but a failure. This result, too, would carry with it a most comprehensive moral. If Grant and his army could do nothing, it is scarcely conceivable that any other Northern army could do better, and the conclusion must be plain that the great object of the Federals — the capture of Richmond — is absolutely unattainable.

Quite unattainable. In fact, never has been attained. Rumors to the contrary, were chaff thrown to the swine of "an American democracy."

As the war approached its close the British papers became week by week more brilliant upon the situation of military affairs. The events are so recent and the opinion expressed as to the course which they would, i. e., which they should take, that no remark is necessary to guide the reader's attention to the full enjoyment of the latter.

GENERAL GRANT'S UNFORTUNATE OPERATIONS.

(From the *London Times*, September 8, 1864.)

"It is an unfortunate characteristic of General Grant's operations that the more closely they are viewed the less satisfactory they appear. The second report of one of his battles is invariably worse than the first, making his losses greater and his achievements smaller than they were originally supposed to be. What was his design at Deep Bottom seems to have been unknown even in New York; but we are now assured, after the usual fashion, that at that place and on the Weldon Railway he lost in a single week 12,000 men. The results, meanwhile, are so absolutely unimportant that General Lee treats the Federal army with perfect unconcern, and not only despatches large reinforcements to Atlanta, but marches away himself, if we may believe the report, at the head of a formidable corps. The Confederate commander is now said to be in the Shenandoah Valley; and it is reasonable, therefore, to look for important intelligence from that quarter. The Southern army already in those parts, under the command of General Early, comprises some 30,000 of the best troops in the service of the Confederacy, and if these are reinforced by other divisions under General Lee himself, and opposed only by Sheridan and his levies, it seems natural to anticipate some decisive operations. [Well, Phil, Sheridan took care that such reasonable anticipations were not disappointed. To permit 30,000 of the best troops in the service of the Confederacy, to say nothing of other divisions, to come out against him and "his levies" for nothing, would not have been handsome. He took care to have some decisive operations; and the *Times* was right.] Nothing, indeed, can be more extraordinary than the position to which affairs have been brought by the course of the campaign. General Grant has reached Richmond, has skirted it by a flank movement, has left it behind him, and is now engaged in some unintelligible operations a few miles south of a small town, itself some miles south of the Confederate capital. [Quite unintelligible: in fact not to be comprehended by the British mind and therefore to be swept out with other muck into the dust-heaps.] General Lee, after first protecting Richmond with his army, now apparently considers it able to protect itself; and has marched away to the North, with a view either of threatening Washington or of carrying the war into the Federal States. [Why, " or "? Why the modest doubtful disjunctive conjunction? We all know that Richmond protected not only itself, but Charleston, Savannah and Wilmington; and that General Lee took Washington and overran "the Federal States."]

THE TIMES OWN WAR CORRESPONDENCE.

One of the chief glories of the *Times* during the war, was its correspondents. Their letters were not only so long and so frequent, but they gave its readers such full and exact information as to the course of events; they were written in such a candid and courteous spirit; and above all they forecasted the immediate future with such sagacity, that by reading the *Times* with sufficient credulity you might generally know exactly what would not happen. Of the two correspondents, one in New York the other in Richmond, it is difficult to say which bore the palm; but perhaps the following performance by the latter worthy, in reference to the campaign which began in the middle — Atlanta, and left off at both ends, — Nashville and Fort McAllister, may be regarded as the most dazzling success the *Times* achieved. It is dated October 8, 1864.

(From the *London Times'* own Richmond Cor.espondent, Oct. 8, 1864.)

It must be known to your readers before the arrival of this letter that President Davis has just returned to Richmond, after a visit to Georgia. The result of his business is that General Beauregard is put in command of the whole of the South-west of the Confederacy on this side of the Mississippi, just as General Lee is in command of Virginia and North Carolina. It must be owned that the arduous task assigned to General Beauregard is "*periculosæ plenum opus aleæ;*" but my belief is that, of all men in the Confederacy, he is, after General Lee, the fittest for the place. . . . . . Moreover, there attaches to Beauregard, as there attached to Stonewall Jackson, a kind of electric popularity which is of wonderful value to a general who commands mercurial and undisciplined soldiers like these Confederates. His name will be to Hood's army a tower of strength; the advantage of consulting with him on all strategical questions will be greatly prized by Hood; and I anticipate from the union of Beauregard and Hood as many advantages as are popularly attributed in the North to the union of Grant and Meade. But the visit of Mr. Davis to Georgia has elevated the *morale* of Hood's army in other ways. . . — . Above all things, he has raised the spirit of Hood's army; he has taught it to entertain misgivings as to the policy of always falling back, and has reconciled it to its present manly and enterprising commander. Nor is the reward which this hitherto unsuccessful army is likely to reap far distant or long deferred. '[Truthful prediction! That army got its deserts without any unreasonable delay.] I have the best authority for saying that the boldest move which has as yet been attempted in this war — the move by which Hood threw his army from the south to the north of Atlanta, and fixed his claws upon the line of Sherman's communications — is of Hood's sole origination. [Which is a comfortable assurance for General Hood.] It remains to be seen whether, in the event of Sherman's adopting almost the only course which seems open to him — I mean in the event of his attacking Hood behind his intrenchments — the much abused Confederate army of the West will strike a blow which, if successful, will do more to end the war than dozens of such battles as were fought in 1861 and 1862. It is my belief that Hood's army, inspirited by the manifest sagacity which is disclosed in the move which it has just made, will prove itself worthy of its vigorous young commander, and will gain for itself and for him a reputation which will eclipse the comparative failures of three and a half years. [Eclipse them? Certainly it eclipsed them. The failures of the previous three and a half years were not to be named in comparison with those by which General Hood gained the reputation with which he closed the war.] If ever there was a war in which *l'audace, l'audace, toujours l'audace* should be the motto of Southern generals, it is the war in which we are here engaged. The two most successful generals of this war — Stonewall Jackson and Lee — are the rashest; and the present promising and daring move of Hood will prove (unless I am mistaken,) before October has closed, that it is only by rashness that telling and staggering blows can be dealt.

The details of the movement by which Hood described well-nigh three-fourths of a circle, and swung his army round Sherman, are described to me as having been very skillfully executed. [Quite correct. No doubt they were skillfully performed; for they were performed just as General Sherman meant they should be. Could there be higher praise?]

But still it would not do for the New York man to allow himself to be entirely eclipsed; and therefore this brilliant passage in his letter published November 1, 1864.

(From the London *Times*, November 1, 1864.)

The situation in the Shenandoah Valley does not promise any results more likely to act favorably for Mr. Lincoln. General Sheridan lost 7,000 men in the obstinate battles of the 19th ult., was so crippled as to be unable to follow up his partial success, and acts at this moment strictly on the defensive. He in no way threatens the Confederates, but guards the valley as well as he can, lest Generals Longstreet and Early should resume offensive demonstrations against Washington. The truth as regards General Sherman on the conterminous borders of Alabama, Georgia, Tennessee, and Mississippi is not so easy to ascertain, but it looks as if General Hood had enticed him from Atlanta, drawn him on a wild goose chase toward Chattanooga, cut him off from his base of supplies, and left General Beauregard to pounce upon Atlanta at the favorable moment, and compel the surrender of the scanty garrison left to hold it under General Slocum.

GENERAL SHERMAN'S "RETREAT."

If a New York correspondent must not be cast in the shade by one at Richmond, still less must editorial wisdom be made as foolishness by the inspiration of any correspondent; and the opportunity for an awful display of sapience arose when Sherman turned his back on Hood and Atlanta, and began that famous "retreat" through Georgia to the sea-board.

(From the London *Times*, December 7, 1864.)

The Southern commanders, after the fall of Atlanta, appear to have thrown themselves on General Sherman's communications, and to have believed that by operating on the long line which connects him with the North they could force him to abandon the advantage he has gained, and to retrace his steps through a wild country, where he might be attacked with every possible advantage. With this view it is said that General Hood has taken up a position more than 100 miles to the north-west of the position occupied by General Sherman. The effect upon that bold and able commander does not appear to have been exactly that which was originally contemplated.

No; not as one might say absolutely, strictly, precisely, accurately, to the very letter, mathematically to a hair, or as some people say, to an azimuth; but on the contrary and with most incomprehensible and incredible perverseness, slightly, or somewhat, or rather, or inclining toward what was *not* originally contemplated.

(From the London *Times*, Dec. 7, 1864.)

We have said that in his invasion of Georgia, General Sherman has left behind him in the north-west General Hood, who it is natural to suppose will not be slow to follow in the footsteps of his retreating antagonist. A few days' delay before Macon or Augusta, or before any of the natural obstacles which must be encountered in a march through a wild and trackless country of between three and four hundred miles, would suffice to bring Hood, possessed of much better information, up with Sherman under circumstances which must almost necessarily place the latter between two fires.

It will be strange, indeed, if the army of General Sherman should arrive before Savannah, after such a march conducted under such difficulties, in condition to attack and storm a town so well fortified and so strenuously defended; and, if not, it is difficult to conceive a more embarrassing position than that General Sherman will occupy, with a wasted and weary army, a strong town in his front, and an enemy fighting on his own ground in his rear. *Ibid.*

Poor Sherman, what a situation he was in! And yet, perverse, conceited Yankee that he was, he did not know it, until he saw this article. What a blessing the *Times* newspaper was to Yankee generals; and how invaluable it must have been to British merchants!

(From the London *Times*, Dec. 20, 1864.)

His march is a repetition on a larger scale of the "great strategic movement" by which M'Clellan transferred his army, after his defeat before Richmond, to Harrison's Landing, where it found, "safety," and the Federal gunboats and transports. But the distance between the York and James rivers is not, as in Georgia measured by hundreds of miles. M'Clellan executed his manœuvre successfully, but the campaign itself was a failure. Sherman has undertaken a more desperate operation of the same kind. He must march to the sea, as no Federal flotilla can ascend the Savannah to aid him. His difficulty is one of frequent recurrence in military history, ancient and modern. An invading army must keep open a line of retreat in case of being out-manœuvred or overpowered, or run the risk of destruction or surrender, either fatal to the expedition. The "ten thousand" Greeks were led by Xenophon from the plains of the Euphrates to the shore of the Black Sea, but the enterprise was undertaken by the wreck of an army. The retreat itself is celebrated in history, but it told the world that the invasion of Persia was a ruinous failure. It is possible that Sherman may save as much of his army as he can march to the shore of the Atlantic; but not the less will the invasion of Georgia have been signally defeated.

Sherman did save just exactly as much of his army as he could march to the shore of the Atlantic. And so the military critic was right again. But whether the invasion of Georgia was therefore signally defeated, he has not since decided.

(From the London *Times*, Dec. 20, 1864.)

To the Northern public the sudden movement was represented as a great military operation, intended to continue the campaign by a bold plunge into the enemy's country, to attack Augusta, and destroy the powder works of the Confederate Government. The capture of the city of Savannah was equally part of the plan. Co-operation in an assault of Charleston from the land side was even suggested as possible. [It *was* thought of. But then the Charleston people, in spite of their talk about the last ditch, did not wait for the co-operation.] The real purpose of Sherman was much more simple, yet difficult enough to carry out successfully, as he has discovered. It was to extricate his army from an untenable position by a rapid march to the sea coast and the aid of the Federal fleet. In the first part of his expedition he was so far fortunate that as he advanced he found no enemy before him. But the Southern troops now begin to appear, *and it is by actual, and not successful, encounters with them that his position is made clear.* . . . . In addition to the difficulties presented by the natural features of the country, the temper of the population must also be considered. South Carolina, always dissatisfied and restless under the old Federal Constitution, was the leading State of the present disruption. It was the first to declare the Southern Confederacy, and the first to commence the actual war by the bombardment of Fort Sumter. The successful defence of that fort and the city of Charleston itself against the repeated attacks of the Federal fleet has encouraged the spirit of the people, and no Southern State is more confident of the issue of the struggle. Taking the country and the population together, it is impossible to predict for General Sherman a progress through it so easy as he has found his march to its frontier.

Even the Northern press cannot persist in representing Sherman's desperate march as a deliberate and skilfully-calculated military operation. We believe it was not a calculation, but a necessity. Sherman had no choice, except of difficulties, long before he quitted Atlanta.

Well, for a chooser of difficulties commend us to General Sherman.

As usual, Richmond and London were completely at accord. They took the same view of Sherman's movement, — spoke of it in the same terms. They both had "taken stock" in the rebellion. But the Richmond people did not pretend to be neutral, or the Richmond editor to be impartial. The following sweeping declaration was made in a leading Richmond paper, almost a month after the appearance of the foregoing judgments in the *Times.*

GOOD NEWS FOR THE REBELS PREDICTED.

(From the *Richmond Whig,* March 8, 1865.)

Sherman is played out. If our readers do not hear or read of any good news from South Carolina, it is a *non sequitur* that there is none to communicate.

In a few days they will hear where Sherman is, and what has befallen him. Let everybody be patient. Sherman's opportunity to establish a military reputation has fled, and we will soon hear of his discomfiture and disgrace.

The last " opinion as was an opinion " upon the military aspect of the war appeared in the columns of the London *Morning Herald* in the letter of its New York correspondent, the worthy successor of "Manhattan," who, writing under appropriate date of April 1st 1865, thus delivered himself upon Grant's last movement before Petersburg.

(From the *Morning Herald*, April 1, 1865.)

The movement had scarcely begun when fighting occurred; its result, we are told, is a Confederate repulse. Be this as it may, the elements are now doing battle for the Confederacy. Scarcely had the hosts of Grant abandoned their encampments when a heavy rain storm set in, which has continued without intermission ever since. Grant's position is one of extraordinary peril. If he has made a mistake, it will, in all probability, result in fearful disaster to the Federal army. If he has not made a mistake, and the Confederates are falling back upon Lynchburg, all the damage he can inflict upon the foe will not compensate him for his trouble, or the risks he runs. It will consist at the most of the capture or the killing and wounding of a few soldiers in the Confederate rear guard, while every step he takes really throws him further and further from his base, and endangers the safety of Washington. Let Grant once place the Confederate army between his force and the national capital, and Washington is lost. If he follows Lee to Lynchburg, Washington is in equal danger; for the Confederates will have the shortest and least obstructed road into Maryland . . . . . Mr. Seward, with much pomposity, has gone down to City Point, inviting several foreign ministers to accompany him to witness the final overthrow of the " rebellion," and the capture of

Richmond. If Grant is defeated, the Secretary will probably return to Washington in a state of complete humiliation. And Grant's defeat is by no means improbable. The army of the Potomac never yet made a successful movement. By taking the initiative, and abandoning his breastworks, Grant gives to Lee an enormous advantage. A Federal defeat, under the present circumstances, means the destruction of the greater portion of the Federal army. There is no coöperation between Sherman and Grant. . . . . Grant's movement, then, is at variance with his original plan of combination. It was forced upon him — he believed that the Confederates were evacuating Richmond, and he wished to strike them when they were outside their earthworks. If he has committed an error, and a battle takes place, his defeat is almost certain. The most probable sequel of the matter will be that the Federal army will return to its old encampments, " the objects of the reconnoissance having been fully accomplished."

Before this letter was well on its way across the Atlantic Richmond was in the possession of that General who was in such "extraordinary peril;" and before it was laid before the sympathetic eyes for which it was written, General Lee had laid down his arms.

FEELING TOWARD DEMOCRATIC GOVERNMENT.

That a contempt for democratic government, and consequent ill will toward one under which a nation had risen to a notable height of prosperity and power was one of the chief motives, if not the chief motive, for the course pursued by the British sympathizers with the rebellion was often manifested during the war. It appeared in such remarks as those in the following paragraph from the London *Times* in regard to the course which our Government was expected to take, but which it did not take, upon the Trent affair.

> If we had to deal with any other than a democracy we should have no doubt upon the matter. It would be impossible for any Monarch to deny a reparation which all the civilized world has declared to be just, for he would feel his personal honor tarnished by such a war. To a democracy the same appeal cannot be made.

Thus the *Times* set up the honor of such perfectly candid, truth telling gentlemen as the Czar Nicholas, Emperor Francis Joseph of Austria, and the Emperor Louis Napoleon, against that of Abraham Lincoln, who told his countrymen that he would resign his office rather than at their bidding break his word to one negro slave, and who lost not his office but his life chiefly because of his good faith in this matter. It would seem as if British experience of the value of "the personal honor" of "a monarch" in the persons of the three potentates above named, — not to go further back into history, might have awakened a suspicion that possibly it was not so very much higher than that of a mere honest man acting as the representative of a great Anglo Saxon people. But it seems quite impossible to convince men who have been accustomed to regard a monarch and an aristocracy as essential elements of any government worthy of the name, that a country in which the people govern themselves through executive officers of their own choice can be anything else than a mere stamping ground of an irresponsible, brutal mob, lawless and resistless, and compelling its representatives to yield to its momentary caprices. Thus speaks the *Times* upon this subject.

(From the London *Times*, Dec. 17, 1861.)

No wonder that Mr. Lincoln, luxuriating in the Paradise to which *the will of an unbridled democracy* has introduced him, and looking forward to a desperate struggle with England, brought about apparently by the same cause, should feel a pious horror of those who venture to think such experience not conclusive, and the existing Constitution of the United States a little short of perfection! We have nothing to say for Slavery, but if Mr. Lincoln's description of the South is indeed true, — if she is fighting to emancipate herself from the *blind tyranny of a degraded mob*, from elective judges and elective governors, — he has given his antagonists a better title to European sympathy than they have hitherto possessed, and thrown upon his Government the stigma of fighting to impose upon others institutions which have already brought it to the verge of ruin.

The Tory journals of course took this same ground, and in language hardly less studiously offensive. The *Morning Herald* is spoken of by many persons as an insignificant paper — the mere organ of the Carleton Club of London. But in the following paragraph it merely puts in another shape the feeling which in the passage just quoted found expression in the ablest, most widely read, and most influential of all British journals.

(From the *Morning Herald*, Feb. 4, 1862.)

Whatever may have been the original merits of the quarrel; — . . . . . It is scarcely possible to doubt that both the world at large and the inhabitants of the Southern States in particular, are likely to be great gainers by the permanent disruption of the Union. *The Americans had become a nuisance among na-*

tions. The enormous growth of their population, the prodigious extent of their territory, inspired them with a wholly disappropriate idea of their own power, dignity, and national capacity. They had bullied Austria, England, and even France, and had not been punished — they naturally believed that they might continue to commit offences against international law and courtesy with the same impunity. The secession of the South completely alters their position. They have now a powerful neighbor and a vulnerable frontier. They are still strong enough to repel aggression; but they can no longer have that overweening confidence in their own strength, that sense of perfect security from consequences, which has made them hitherto the most aggressive of nations.

This about a people who have never interfered with any other nation; who have only asked that others should not insult and brow-beat them; who have never troubled themselves about the balance of power, or set themselves up as the guardians of civilization!

How nearly some of the best educated and ablest writers for the British press can approach to a just appreciation of the national characteristics and the public policy of our Republic, is shown by the following extract from an article in the *Saturday Review* in which the consequences to us of our war against the Confederate slaveholders are gravely considered.

(From the *Saturday Review*, Aug. 31, 1864.)

A first rate general at the head of such an army as will be necessary to conquer and subjugate even a fraction of the seceding States will be incomparably the most powerful and popular man in America : and *it will be entirely by his own choice if he ever subsides into private life.* . . . . Meanwhile the danger that threatens their favorite democratic institutions are contemplated by Americans with an easy indifference which is rather startling. . . . . Nothing in America seems to follow the ordinary laws of human nature!

Fudge, O wise man, fudge! Fudge, not so much on account of your most ridiculous blunder in regard to the successful General; but because it is useless to waste words with a man who does not see that here in this republic the laws of human nature have for the first time had something like freedom of operation.

SPIRIT AND PURPOSE OF THE REBELLION.

The spirit and purpose of the rebellion might be illustrated in a general way by multitudinous extracts from newspapers in its interest, and from public documents issued by the government of the so called Confederacy, in addition to those given above; but the following passages, consigning General Butler and his officers to the gallows, and all the negroes in the United States army to the same fate, justifying Quantrell's murderous raid into Kansas, recommending that our soldiers, taken prisoners, should be starved and frozen to death, and proposing the re-establishment of the slave-trade, answer the purpose as well as if they were more numerous.

MR. DAVIS'S PROCLAMATION IN REGARD TO GENERAL BUTLER, NEGRO SOLDIERS AND OFFICERS IN COMMAND OF THEM.

First — That all the commissioned officers in the command of said Benjamin F. Butler be declared not entitled to be considered as soldiers engaged in honorable warfare, but as robbers and criminals deserving death; and that they and each of them be, whenever captured, reserved for execution.

Second — That the private soldiers and non-commissioned officers in the army of said Butler be considered as only the instruments used for the commission of crimes perpetrated by his orders, and not as free agents; that they, therefore, be treated when captured as prisoners of war, with kindness and humanity, and be sent home on the usual parole that they will in no manner aid or serve the United States in any capacity during the continuance of this war, unless duly exchanged.

Third — That all negro slaves captured in arms be at once delivered over to the executive authorities of the respective States to which they belong, to be dealt with according to the laws of said States.

Fourth — That the like orders be executed in all cases with respect to all commissioned officers of the United States when found serving in company with said slaves in insurrection against the the authorities of the different States of this Confederacy.

In testimony whereof I have signed these presents and caused the seal of the Confederate States of America to be affixed thereto, at the City of Richmond, on this 23d day of December, in the year of our Lord one thousand eight hundred and sixty-two.

By the President,   JEFFERSON DAVIS.
J. P. Benjamin, Secretary of State.

NEWSPAPER COMMENTS.

On this proclamation the Richmond *Despatch* has the following comments:

"The proclamation against Butler and his associates comes up to the full measure of public expectation. The deliberation with which the conclusions of the Executive have been arrived at gives additional solemnity and dignity to his purpose. The brute and his minions will discover that it does not follow because sentence against an evil work is not executed speedily that it is forgotten or forgiven.

THE RAID ON KANSAS JUSTIFIED

(From the *Richmond Examiner*, Sept. 1863.)

The accounts of Quantrell's retreat are as little worthy of belief as those of his conduct at Lawrence. According to these accounts his command scattered, and eighty of his men have been overtaken and put to death in cold blood. That Lane and his horde of miscreants have indeed seized and murdered eighty citizens of Missouri in cold blood, is quite probable; but that they were Quantrell's men is not at all probable. *The expedition to Lawrence was a gallant and perfectly fair blow at the enemy*, but as it fell heavy upon him, and as the population of Kansas is malignant and scoundrelly beyond description, no doubt can be entertained that it will be made the excuse and pretext of every species of atrocity in Missouri, until the confederate leaders do what they ought to have done, and what they are falsely accused of doing. A resort to *lex talionis* in its most decisive form is the only hope of safety in Missouri, as it soon will be everywhere.

STARVING OF PRISONERS RECOMMENDED.

(From the *Richmond Examiner*, Oct. 20.)

The proper authorities are debating the question of the removal of the twelve thousand Yankee prisoners from Richmond to some other point not so circumscribed for food, and where it can be had at less expense and at greater abundance, without affecting the necessities of the people. Danville, or some location on the James River Canal, is spoken of. We are glad the question has been started, and the citizens of Richmond will do all in their power to help them to a decision.

The Yankee Government, under the laws of civilized warfare and the cartel, are entitled to these men, and if they will not take them, *let them be put where the cold weather and scant fare will thin them out in accordance with the laws of nature.*

OPENING OF THE SLAVE TRADE RECOMMENDED

The Richmond *Enquirer* of November 10th, 1863, noticing some remarks in *L'Opinion Nationale,* upon Mr. Slidell's unwillingness to discuss the subject of slavery, said: —

Neither is this a matter of temper, and pride, and passion alone. Far from it. Let the *Opinion* know also — and let it take what further comfort and aid it can from the avowal — that the Confederate people calmly and considerately prefer their social and industrial institutions to those of any other land — that our consciences are easy about them — that we believe those institutions supply us with that just and humane balance between capital and labor, which society in Europe so deeply needs, and which the Editor of the *Opinion* and his associates sought in their various theories of communism, but never found and never will. Finally, let him understand that if our system of labor needs now, or, should come to need, what they call 'amelioration,' we mean to be the sole judges and the sole administrators thereof; although, indeed, as at present advised, we can conceive no amelioration at all, save, perhaps, in the copious importation of more negroes from Africa.

The foregoing passages fully bear out Mr. Cobden in his assertions in the following passage taken from a speech at Rochdale, November, 24, 1863, and the event of the war has entirely justified its faith in the strength of virtue and freedom.

(From Mr. Cobden's *Rochdale Speech.*)

This is a war to extend and perpetuate human Slavery. It is a war not to defend Slavery as it was left by their ancestors — a thing to be retained, and to be apologized for. It is a war to establish a slave empire, where Slavery shall be made the corner-stone of the social system, where it shall be defended and justified on scriptural and ethnological grounds. I say God pardon the men who in this year of grace, 1863 should think that such a project as that should be crowned with success. Now you know why I have from the first never believed it possible that the South could succeed, and I have not founded that faith merely on moral instincts which teach us to repudiate the idea that anything so infernal should succeed. No. *It is because in this world the virtues and the forces go together, and the vices and weakness are inseparable. It is, therefore, I felt certain that this project never could succeed.* For how is it? Here is a community with nearly half of the population slaves, and they are attempting to fight another community where every working man is a free man.

* * * *I say it is an aristocratic rebellion against a democratic Government.* That is the title I would give to it. In all history, when you have had the aristocracy pitted against the people in a physical force and conflict, the aristocracy have always gone down under the heavy blows of the democracy.

SAGACITY.

John Bull seems to try so hard to trace the course of public opinion in the United States, and he has such a very wise head upon his shoulders, that it would seem as if with all his effort he must be able to understand what so very simple and outspoken a people as we are, mean. What his success is in a general way, we know; what it was in regard to our views upon the rebellion, the following passages will show.

THE IRRESISTIBLE PEACE MOVEMENT.

(From the *London Times,* Special Correspondence, Aug. 27, 1864.)

The revulsion of feeling in favor of peace is one of the most extraordinary of all the incidents of the war. It would seem as if the idea had long been latent in everybody's mind, and that there only wanted some one to give it authoritative expression, to send it round the country with the all-subduing power of a mania or an epidemic.

* * * * * * *

In nine days from this time—*i. e.*, on the 5th of September, if there be no armistice in the interval, — Mr. Lincoln must enforce, or begin to enforce, his last call for half a million of men. It is understood that his friends and supporters, who desire his re-election for their own purposes if not for his or the public benefit, have urged upon him the expediency of letting the matter drop until the election shall have been decided, and that Mr. Lincoln is unconvinced by their reasoning.

* * * * * * *

If these statements of the President's feeling and intentions be correct he must either accept the popular idea of an armistice and a convention, or risk the perils of an insurrection in attempting to enforce a measure, the exigencies of which the rich and well to do throw upon foreign mercenaries and negroes, and which the poor detest and abhor, and *will fight in the streets to resist.* The indications are that the question will be decided at Chicago. If Chicago be for war there will be a draught; if Chicago be for peace, *as there is every probability that it will be, not simply by an overwhelming majority, but by unanimity,* it is difficult to see how the Administration can run a risk of a conscription, which, under the circumstances, would be as unnecessary in itself as it would be distasteful to all classes.

(From the *London Times* of Sept. 8th, 1864.)

A broad view of this kind is all that can be taken of these remarkable events. The more secret views of parties are of course hidden from us. We can only tell at this moment that the party or aggregate of parties desirous of suspending the war and substituting amicable negotiation is strong enough to compel others, with more or less sincerity, to accept its policy. It seems by no means improbable that the policy of an armistice will be adopted even by Mr. Lincoln himself, so that *in any event the Presidential election would bring the close of hostilities for the present.* Then follows a mighty question :— Will the war ever be renewed? If the South should refuse, on any terms, to reënter the Union, will the Northern people, who now admit that the war has brought them no good, recur to that arbitrament in hopes of better fortune? Perhaps a majority of them would profess that intention at the present moment; but to us, on this side of the Atlantic, it seems very difficult to imagine that two Governments which have had such bitter experience of war should ever deliberately renew it after a taste of peace.

For the first time, however, during the whole of this contest, we are brought within sight of its probable end, and it is curious to reflect with what suddenness the prospect has at last arisen. Beyond doubt the convictions which it expresses must have long been gaining strength in the minds of the Northern people, but still they found little utterance till the other day. That they are now proclaimed so loudly is due to the double opportunity presented by the Presidential election and the acknowledged failure of the last campaign.

In the meantime the political campaign is far more eventful and invested with far more immediate interest. There the issue cannot be delayed, nor the contest indefinitely prolonged. A few days, indeed, will now bring us a most important, if not decisive, piece of intelligence. On the 29th of August a Democratic candidate for the Presidency was nominated at Chicago, and that nomination will, in all probability, govern the election, and with it the course of the war. It may be observed, too, that as we have war news at this moment up to the 27th ult. we may regard it as certain that neither Grant nor Sherman nor Farragut could have achieved anything likely to influence the proceedings of the Convention in favor of the war party. The support which Mr. Lincoln and the partisans might possibly have derived from the capture of Atlanta or Mobile is now past hoping for, and the resolutions of the great political meeting will have been taken on the assumption that the campaign of 1864 will end as unprofitably for the North as those of the years proceeding. That last chance for the Republicans has been lost, and the misgivings of the party may be clearly discerned in the proposition now reported, that Mr. Lincoln and General Fremont should retire together, and make way for some new candidate for the Presidency more popularly acceptable than either. Everything now tends in the direction of peace, or, at any rate, towards the suspension of war; and the Americans appear to be embracing this new policy of negotiation with the same impulse which first hurried them into civil conflict.

It must not be supposed that the Northern people have yet accepted the idea of Southern independence, or relinquished the hope of restoring the Union. All they have learnt at present is that the Union is not to be restored by war.

THE TIMES WISHES NOT TO BE MISUNDERSTOOD, AND IS NOT.

(From the *London Times*, September 14, 1864.)

The Chicago Convention has not only declared the principles on which the Democratic party is prepared to act, but has demanded, in the name of the people, that negotiations shall be immediately instituted for the suspension of arms. An Armistice at once, a Conference as soon as possible — these are the cries now resounding through the States of the North; and unless they can be disregarded — which is not easy to suppose — we may relieve ourselves from the trouble of further speculations on the events of the war.

We trust the public will admit that they have not been misguided by our comments on this obstinate contest. The great fact WHICH WE ASSERTED FROM THE FIRST *is now placed beyond reach of controversy.* WE SAID THAT THE NORTH COULD NEVER SUBDUE THE SOUTH, and the North has now proclaimed the same conclusion. After three years of the most desperate efforts, in which no expenditure has been spared and no tactics have been left untried, a preponderating section of the Northern people have put on record before the world their deliberate conviction that the policy of war is mistaken and hopeless, and that it must be superseded by a policy of conciliation and compromise.

* * * * * * *

The questions now before us are written in broad and unmistakable characters. First, will the actual Government accede to the demand expressed by the Chicago Convention for an immediate Armistice? And, next, will the South accept the Armistice and enter upon the subsequent Conference on any basis except that of national independence? As regards the former of these inquiries, the world has been much misled if the Democratic party is not the strongest party in the Northern States — strong enough, in the absence of any unexpected events, to carry in November next its candidate for Presidency, and to impress its policy in the interval upon the existing Administration. It is hardly to be conceived that President Lincoln would employ his brief remaining term of office in counteracting or opposing the declared will of the majority of his countrymen. We regard the Chicago Convention as representing a majority of the people, because it has been asserted throughout that the Democratic party, if united, could easily outnumber all opponents; and they are perfectly united now.

As the *Times* remarked in regard to Hood's attempt upon Sherman's communications, the effect in this case was not exactly what was expected. The Chicago Convention did not adopt a peace *and* disunion policy; and nevertheless the nominees of that Convention were beaten as never men were beaten before. What then does the thunderer do? It confesses a fact which cannot be denied, but it seeks to blacken Mr. Lincoln's character by impugning the motives of the measures which he took to secure a fair election in Tennessee and Louisiana, and to avoid the consequences of his re-election by opening a way to the denial of the legality of his title as President of the entire Union under his second election, as follows.

The acts of fraud and of violence which might have been found useful in a close contest proved to be superfluous, except as far as they gratified the popular taste for ostensible vigor. Mr. Lincoln was re-elected by so great a majority of genuine votes that he could have afforded to abstain from all irregular arrangements. No President has been unequivocally the choice of the constituency which elected him: but the States which were bound as a minority by the lawful election of 1860, are utter strangers to a vote taken in their absence in 1864.

And yet, after a paragraph like this, to say nothing of others which have been quoted before, the *Times* begins its very next sentence.

The spectacle of the troubles in the United States, and the blustering menaces of the Northern populace and its leaders, &c. &c. &c. &c.

Mr. J. B. is of course to have a monopoly of menace as well as of bluster.

GENERAL BRAG AND BLUSTER.

A close examination of the newspapers of the Free States discovers that, with the exception of those edited in the interests of the rebels, most of them, and in fact all of any importance, exhibited what, under the circumstances, was a remarkable moderation of tone during the war. They denounced rebellion and slavery with little reserve; but of rebels and slave-holders they said nothing that was insulting, and comparatively little that was derogatory. Of the manner in which the people of the Free States were spoken of by the rebel and the principal British journals, the following passages are examples. They come under no particular head, and may be properly ranged under that of General Brag, Bluster, Vituperation, and Misrepresentation.

(From the London *Times*, Sept. 12, 1861.)

Yet, both the New Englanders and the New Yorkers are right. If the trick be not quickly done it cannot be done at all. It is very well for England and France to go on ostentatiously contending which can throw most money into the sea, but there are a thousand obvious reasons why this will not do for America. This golden goose is not to be killed, it must be taken alive; but the process must be very speedy. Even during the short time that has elapsed the symptoms are of a very grave character. They go to the very existence of society in North America. We say nothing to the sacrifice of free institutions, nothing to the surrender of individual liberty, nothing to the establishment of the futile precautions of despotism. We do not make a point of the abolition of *habeas corpus*, or the introduction of passports, nor of the suppression of obnoxious newspapers, nor of the imprisonment of ladies suspected of writing postscripts to their letters, and certainly not of the numerous cases of gentlemen of unpopular politics being made to ride out of town upon a rail. So free a country as America can afford to dispense with all the safeguards of individual liberty necessary to a mere monarchy; and King Mob where he is supreme will naturally require the same agents as any single tyrant. Unfortunately, however, for King Mob, while a single tyrant can only eat and drink a single bellyful, King Mob's hunger and thirst can only be appeased by many millions of bellyfuls. There is poverty in New York, and there is hunger already in New England.

And this was written three years and more before the insurrection was put down.

(From the London *Times*, Nov. 7, 1861.)

There is no misapprehension as to our opinions. We do believe, and shall continue to do so, that the Secession of the South has destroyed the Federal Union, and that, to whichever side victory incline, its reconstruction on the old basis is impossible, for the simple reason that the Southern States, if conquered, cannot be treated as equals in political power to the Northern, and that without such equality a return to the former state of things is impossible. We also think that, as revolution is inevitable, it had better come in the form which would most speedily arrest the effusion of blood.

There can indeed be no misapprehension as to these opinions; no more than there can be as to the value which events have set upon their worth. With the Republic preserved in its integrity, and every commonwealth in it standing already on an absolute political equality with every other, with the great mass of the people who were lately rebels in arms restored to their civil and political rights, while those most responsible for the rebellion are relieved of their political disabilities and of the other consequences of their political crime almost as rapidly as they will ask for such relief, such opinions as those above quoted are only amusing to their readers.

(From the *Saturday Review* of Nov. 12th, 1861.)

England may ultimately be obliged to say to the Northern States — " Your conduct is so injurious to others as well as yourselves — your extravagant and prolonged exercise of the severest belligerent rights, and the enormous dimensions which you have given to the theory of blockade, inflict so much misery on the innocent, and cause such intolerable vexations to the commerce of the whole civilized world — that the continuance of our neutrality is practically impossible, and we will take part with the Southern Ststes for the purpose of bringing to a conclusion a disastrous and otherwise interminable war." Even if England, from whatever motives of prudence or magnanimity, should pertinaciously refuse to take this step, she could not prevent France from taking it, and from being hailed as the peacemaker of the great American continent.

(From the *Saturday Review* of Dec. 7th, 1861.)

The American naval adventurer has plenty of shrewdness, of resource, and of *that kind of courage which kindles at the prospect of pocketing another person's dollars.*
We have also rather left out of view the Warrior and her sister ship, because, although it might be highly desirable to test the seaworthiness of these vessels by making them part of a blockading squadron, we can scarcely suppose that the American navy would approach near enough even to give them a chance of displaying their enormous speed. We never heard in the last war that the Constitution ran into the midst of our Channel fleet; and we do not expect that any one of her modern sisters will offer herself as a customer for the Warrior. *The tactics of the American navy have always been, and will be still, entirely guiltless of rash adventure.* We know well what those tactics would be, and, in the deplorable event of war, it will be our own fault if they take us unprepared.

After this was published the naval battle below New Orleans took place, resulting in the capture of the city, and in which Admiral Farragut's fleet dashed into such a pandemonium of forts, fire-ships, fire-rafts and gun-boats, as was never seen before, and was victorious; one ship, the *Varina*, sinking five of her opponents before she sunk herself. After this, too, Farragut captured the forts in Mobile harbor, standing in the main-top of his wooden ship. Yet the *Saturday Review* will look in vain for any retraction or modification of the above assertions.

(From a *Speech by Mr. Jefferson Davis before the Mississipi Legislature*, Dec. 26, 1861.)

I was among those who, from the beginning predicted war as the consequence of secession, *although I must admit that the contest has assumed proportions more gigantic than I had anticipated.* I predicted war, not because our right to secede and to form a Government of our own was not indisputable and clearly defined in the spirit of that declaration which rests the right to govern on the consent of the governed, but saw that the wickedness of the North would precipitate a war upon us. Those who supposed that the exercise of this right of separation could not produce war, have had cause to be convinced that they had credited their recent associates of the North with a moderation, a sagacity, a morality, they did not possess. *You have been involved in a war waged for the gratification of the lust of power and aggrandizement, for your conquest and your subjugation, with a malignant ferocity and with a disregard and a contempt of the usages of civilization entirely unequalled in history. Such, I have ever warned you, were the characteristics of the Northern people* — of those with whom our ancestors entered into a Union of consent, and with whom they formed a constitutional compact. *After what has happened during the last two years, my only wonder is that we consented to live for so long a time in association with such miscreants, and have loved so much a Government rotten to the core. Were it ever to be proposed again to enter into a Union with such a people, I could no more consent to do it than to trust myself in a den of thieves.*

There is indeed a difference between the two peoples. Let no man hug the delusion that there can be renewed association between them. Our enemies are a traditionless and homeless race; from the time of Cromwell to the present moment they have been disturbers of the peace of the world. Gathered together by Cromwell from the bogs and fens of the North of Ireland and of England, they commenced by disturbing the peace of their own country; they disturbed Holland, to which they fled, and they disturbed England on their return.

Mr. Davis could hardly be so ignorant of history as not to know, that the Hollanders especially admired and praised the Puritans because, during their sojourn in the low countries, they had lived such exemplary peacefully lives. As to their disturbance of England, he knew well that to that we, as well as the mother country, owe the freedom, the happiness, and the prosperity which distinguishes us from all other peoples.

(From the London *Times* July 9th, 1862.)

But what a destiny are these degenerate and insensate people preparing for themselves? They are not shutting themselves out from all mankind in order to work out some philosophic dream of peace and innocence. They have not even the short-sighted wisdom of the Chinese or the Japanese, who, in their happy conceit, feared to be contaminated by outside intercourse. These people are isolating themselves *only in order that they may indulge their own fierce vices uncontrolled.* With this object they are reducing themselves to a condition which is a warning to the world. They have at last actually taken upon themselves a system of taxation which is like the cask of Regulus, so full of points that no man can stand, or sit, or lie in it without being pricked every moment.

That's the way of course. First abuse the Yankees for not taxing themselves; say that they will rather repudiate their debts than bear taxation to pay them; and then when they do tax themselves thoroughly, and submit to the sacrifice cheerfully, abuse them for doing what you said they would not do.

(From the London *Times* July 9, 1862.)

At home no man's life, or liberty, or property is secure, for how can life or liberty be secure in a country where the Habeas Corpus Act is suspended indefinitely, where citizens have no redress against unlawful imprisonment, and no available means of obtaining a public trial; and how can property be secure when money is no longer a thing of intrinsic value, and when confiscation and taxation are becoming words of similar meaning? This is the happy Union which the Americans are now making for themselves, and to which they expect that, when it is completed, all mankind will flock. They have but to add to it, as they are now doing, the abnegation of all the comforts of civilized life, and they will soon have to negotiate a Fugitive Slave law with their neighbors to keep their own subjects within their pale.

Here's wisdom, here's forecast. The whole world knows that as this sort of thing was kept up for more than two years after this judgment was pronounced, the entire population of the Free States fled to Canada, and emigration ceased entirely.

(From the London *Times*, July 9, 1862.)

The broken States of North America seem to be fast approaching that point when they must become two reasonable nations, or go on to anarchy and dissolution.

So spoke the London *Times* in the summer of 1862. At the same period, in the same month, like words were uttered by the organs of the rebellion at Richmond, as appears by the following example, from the Richmond *Enquirer*.

(From the *Richmond Enquirer* of July, 1862.)

When peace has once returned, it will be but a short time before a storm will break over the United States, if not as destructive to life and fortune as the present war, at least as ruinous to national union. Another disruption of territory, another secession will break out, severing the grain-growing free trade West from manufacturing New England.

This is truly alarming. How we are going to re-establish the connection between the East and West passes our humble understanding. If the London *Times* and the Richmond *Enquirer* would just lay their heads together and give us a little sound, friendly, and disinterested — yes, that's the word, — disinterested advice, we possibly might learn something.

(From the *London Times*, of July 22, 1862.)

Will nothing arrest this frantic and suicidal rage? Is there no one from whom the American people will listen to the words of truth and soberness? We know that counsels of moderation, ever distasteful in themselves, are doubly distasteful when coming from us, but we can scarcely believe that the infuriated multitude will remain as blind to the teaching of facts as they have hitherto been deaf to the voice of well meant expostulation. What proof do they yet require that they are embarked on a fatal and ruinous cause? *Their wealth is turned into poverty, their peace into discord, their prosperity into wretchedness; the power in which they gloried is effaced; society is torn in pieces by its own members; law is trampled under foot, and the country is fast falling into anarchy, the only refuge from which is despotism.* We do not scruple to say we shall rejoice if the worst anticipation shall be realized — not from any ill will to the North, but because we see in the failure of its efforts to subjugate the Southern states the only prospect — we had almost said the only possibility — of Peace.

"TOWSER" AGAIN.

(From Mr. Roebuck's Sheffield Speech, May 26, 1863.)

But the North themselves, from the very commencement, so determined on empire — they forgot Christianity; *they made themselves a spectacle to the world of cruelty, corruption and horror.* The South stood up, like the real descendants, as they are, of Englishmen. They said, "We will vindicate to ourselves the right to govern ourselves; we will fight to the death for our independence." And they have fought to the death. They have conquered the North. I ask myself if the time has come when surrounding nations shall do what we ought to do now—acknowledge the South as an independent nation.

* * * * * * *

Sympathy is not a part of neutrality. I have no sympathy with the North. I think my sympathies ought to go, as they do go, with the South. They are a gallant people, fighting for their independence. and they have obtained it. [Fact, Towser. Can't deny it. Bow wow wow!]

From Gov. Letcher's Message to the Virginia Legislature Jan. 1860.)

It is not marvelous, in view of all these things, that we could so long have remained in association with such a people. This war has exhibited them *in their true characters—as murderers and robbers*. They have disregarded all the rules of civilized warfare. *Their prisoners we take are entitled to no consideration.* [This explains Andersonville.] If they receive their deserts, they would be regularly indicted and tried for violating our State laws, and suffer the penalties which those laws annex to their crimes. The alliance between us is dissolved, never, I trust, to be renewed at any time, or under any conceivable state of circumstances. Let us achieve our independence, as it is certain we will, establish our government upon a firm and enduring basis, develop our material resources, valuable beyond all calculation, and move forward in the highway of greatness and power and influence. When the war ends, a bright and glorious future awaits us.

But it seems to do nothing else but wait.

(From the London *Times* of Feb. 7, 1863.)

"After a recess of six eventful months there is not a single statesman on either side who believes that the restoration of the Union, on the terms of the original compact is possible; not one, who believes that the forcible subjugation of the South is possible, Though there is one who declares that if such a conquest was practicable, it would only prove the political ruin of America. We arrive then at the one conclusion; that separation on peaceable terms and at the earliest moment, is the result which the friends of America ought to desire."

Dear, good, disinterested friends! What a pity they were disappointed.

"CHIVALRIC" MODESTY AND COURTESY.

The spirit in which the slave-mongering editors did their work, and the "style of article" that they had reason to believe would find favor with the most cultivated polished, and, in their own ridiculous phrase, "aristocratic" and "chivalric" communities of the slave holding States, are exhibited by the following typical articles published in the Richmond *Examiner* and the Charleston *Mercury* in the second year of the war.

(From the Richmond *Examiner*, Jan. 26.)

The custom of denouncing the Yankees is becoming common. Under the soft influences of a serenade, President Davis likens them to hyenas; Gov. Letcher, in his mild way, insists that they are a heaven-defying, hell-deserving race, and pleasantly consigns their Chief Magistrate, Abe Lincoln, to a doom more fearful than that of Devergoil. Is it to be wondered that Mr. Lincoln has had a trouble on his mind ever since this fearful doom was pronounced upon him; that he is getting gray, and finds it difficult to tell a dirty anecdote every ten minutes during the day?

The practice of villifying the Yankees has gotten into the newspapers. Editors spend most of their time in concocting diatribes against a contemptible race, whose only defect is a *proneness to all that is foul and everything that is evil.* Why should a people so despicable be aspersed? Even this newspaper, careful as it is never to say a word that would disturb the most placid tea-party, has been known to speak disrespectfully of a race which the civilized world, with one consent, acknowledges to be "*its last and vilest product.*" One would suppose that creatures so abounding in the stenches of moral decomposition, would never be alluded to in decent society. But somehow the habit of expectorating upon the vermin that swarm the Northern dunghill, has gotten the better of gentle natures, and the time drags heavily on the Southerner who refuses to indulge himself some twenty times a day in a volley of direful anathemas against the Yankees.

Reflecting persons tell us that this is altogether wrong. We should restrain ourselves and be scrupulously polite in speaking of these abominable villains. We should recollect that these infernal scoundrels are human beings, and bear in mind the fact that they never lose an opportunity of heaping the most ungracious abuse upon ourselves. Nor should it be forgotten that they have attained an almost inconceivable perfection and dexterity in lying, so that if it were possible for us to match them in billingsgate, we would still be at their mercy in the trifling matter of falsehood. We are told by our philosophic friends that it should serve to cool the intensity of our hatred to remember that they are hourly committing every crime known to man, and some with which even the fiends are not familiar; that a thrill of delight should pass through us, when we recall the pleasing circumstance that upward of a milllion of these incarnate demons are hired by the year for the sole purpose of murdering us, burning our houses, killing our cattle, stealing our slaves, destroying our crops, and driving our wives and helpless children into the waste, howling wilderness, in mid-winter; that a genial glow of the purest love should pervade our hearts at the thought that they candidly avow their purpose to exterminate us, to kill every one of us, men, women and children, to take our possessions by violence: in a word, to annihilate us, to destroy us from the face of the earth, so that our names shall no more be heard among men.

There is another view which should encourage us in the purpose henceforth to cherish an affectionate regard for the accursed beings at war with us. To the well-regulated mind, *the beastly practices of beasts excites no disagreeable emotion;* and it is said that the scientific intellect finds a world of enjoyment in the contemplation of the disgusting utility of the lowest order of creatures. Surely, the feast of the vulture upon carrion is not reprehensible, and occasions in the beholder no special wonder, and never any animosity against the bird for gratifying his somewhat peculiar tastes. *So the tiger that laps blood and the beetle that gorges excrement, are but Yankees of the animal kingdom,* accommodating the wants of nature; and it were folly to impute to them improper motives in partaking of their ghastly and sickening repasts. It follows that our feelings toward the people of the North, the scarabœi and vipers of humanity, should be characterized neither by rage or nausea, but by a fixed, cheerful, Christian determination to interpose sufficient obstacles between them and ourselves; to curb their inordinate and bloody lusts by such adequate means as natural wit suggests, and, as a general thing, to kill them wherever we find them, without idle questions as to whether they are reptiles or vermin. A certain calmness of mind is requisite to their successful slaughter. The convulsions of passion are out of place when one is merely scalding chinches.

(From the Charleston *Mercury.*)

Our women are all conservative, moral, religious, and sensitively modest, and abhor the North for its infidelity, gross immorality, licentiousness, anarchy, and agrarianism. 'Tis they and the clergy who lead and direct the disunion movement. It is a gross mistake to suppose that Abolition alone is the cause of the dissension between the North and the South. The Cavaliers, Jacobites, and Huguenots, who settled the South, naturally hate, contemn, and despise the Puritans, who settled the North. The former are master races — the latter a slave race, the decendants of the Saxon serfs! [This assertion, so often made, is certainly the funniest of all the slaveholders notions. Names tell origin without possibility of error; the identity of surnames North and South affords us no occasion of finding an excuse in difference of race for slaveholding, and for rebellion on account of the loss of an election.]

We are the most aristocratic people in the world. Pride of caste, and color, and privilege, makes every white man an aristocrat in feeling. Aristocracy is the only safeguard of liberty, the only power watchful and strong enough to exclude monarchical despotism. At the North, the progress and tendency of opinion is to pure democracy, less government, anarchy, and agrarianism. Military despotism is far preferable to Northern democracy, agrarianism, infidelity, and free love.

Our enemies, the stupid, sensual, ignorant masses of the North, who are as foolish as they are depraved, could not read the signs of the times, did not dream of disunion, but rushed on as heedlessly as a greedy drove of hungry dogs, at the call of their owners. They were promised plunder, and find a famine; promised bread, and were given a stone. Our enemies are starving and disorganized. The cold, naked, hungry masses, are at war with their leaders; they are mute, paralyzed, panic stricken, and have no plan of action for the future.

Better, a thousand times better, to come under the dominion of free negroes, or of gypsies, than of Yankees, or low Germans, or Canadians. Gypsies and free negroes have many amiable, noble, and generous traits; the Yankees, sour-krout Germans, filthy, whiskey-drinking Irish and Canadians, have none. Senator Wade says, and Seward too, that the North will absorb Canada. They are half true; the vile, sensual, animal, brutal, infidel, superstitious Democracy of Canada and the Yankee States will coalesce: and Senator Johnson of Tennessee, will join them. But when Canada, and Western New York, and New England, and the whole beastly, puritanic, "sour-krout," free negro, filthy, whiskey-drinking Irish, infidel, superstitious, licentious, Democratic population of the North, become masters of New York — what then? Out of the city, the State of New York is Yankee and puritanical, composed of as base, unprincipled, superstitious, licentious, and agrarian and anarchical population, as any on earth. Nay, we do not hesitate to say, it is the vilest population on earth. If the city does not secede and erect a separate Republic, this population, aided by the ignorant, base, brutal, sensual German infidels of the Northwest, the stupid Democracy of Canada, (for Canada will in some way coalesce with the North,) and the arrogant and tyrannical people of New England, will become masters of the destinies of New York."

Equally modest, elegant and true. Coming from the leading journals of the two cities which set themselves up as the pinks of "Southern chivalry," how could it be otherwise? Most absurd and laughable as this entire article is, that notion that the city of New York is the salt and salvation of the State, beats all the rest, especially as there are more "low Germans" and "whiskey-drinking Irish" in it than in all the rest of the country together.

(From the Richmond *Whig* of May 22, 1863.)

It is seen and acknowledged everywhere that the race so maligned and belittled by the writers and speakers whose words reached Europe and formed opinion there concerning us, is *the master race of this continent, with a genius, a civilization and morality far above and in advance of the upstart and vulgar race of the North*, and with a domain richer in production and capabilities than any nation on earth possesses. As these discoveries have been made the corresponding truth has appeared, that the Northern race were wanting in those elements of character from which alone a great people are formed, and in those resources of nature from which national wealth and power flow. Accordingly as we have risen in the estimation of the trans-Atlantic world, the Yankee race has sunk. What we have gained they have lost, and more; for the falsehoods and arrogance of the past now serve to bear down the balances in which they are weighed, until they have reached the level of universal contempt.

And at the level which they have reached they are for the present contented to remain. But is it not too laughable, this everlasting brag about being the master *race*, when there was not a name on their army roll, or their civil list, from Lee and Davis down, that was not as common all over the Free States as blackberries in August?

DOGS VS. YANKEES.

Mr. J. M. McCue, a member of the Virginia House of Delegates, recently addressed a note to a Mr. Ferneyhough, who seems to be a practical tanner, asking his opinion regarding the value of dead dogs from several points of view. He received a reply, from which the following is an extract.

"The immense number of useless dogs to the State would go far toward furnishing a substitute both for making leather and dressing it. The per cent. of all other oils used now in the South, will not amount to five per cent. The value of calf and dog skin leather for ladies' wear, and for summer boots for gentlemen is nearly the same. The value of green calf skins is about double that of dogs. The dog skin is tough, soft, pliable and as nearly equal to kid as any substitute that can be used. The quanity of oil that can be extracted from a medium-sized dog will amount to only one and a half gallons. The carcasses can then make a value ingredient to the nitre beds of the city, as does the offal of the carcasses of horses and cattle referred to. To aid in the all-important object of furnishing the Government with nitre similar beds to those near Richmond ought to be found at every town and village in the State, and the otherwise worthless carcass of the dog can be made available in consigning to the soil of the South as a manure that far more worthless and offensive carcass, viz., the Yankee."

Which is a christian, gentlemanlike, "aristocratic and chivalric" view of the subject.

(From the *Richmond Enquirer, May* 27, 1863.)

The first resolution adopted at a late Peace meeting in New York read thus:

"*Resolved.* That we reiterate our opposition to this bloody, relentless, unnecessary and fruitless war. In our opinion it is time that the whole American people, North and South, should demand of their rulers its immediate discontinuance."

We fear we must say to these peaceable New Yorkers, speak for yourself. They persist in laboring under the mistake that there is a "whole American people;" and that it has certain rulers who are carrying on an unnecessary and fruitless war which they ought immediately to discontinue. This must be set right. Their rulers may be carrying on an unnecessary war, seeing it is a war of invasion and aggression. *Our* rulers are carrying on a war which is absolutely necessary, so long as that invasion continues. Their rulers can discontinue the war when they please. Ours cannot, and dare not so much as hint at its discontinuance. Their war may be fruitless; but ours is bearing and ripening the rich and glorious fruit of freedom and separate independence, and national dignity, and an honorable fame.

It is a fruit that we must rear, indeed, with pains and toil, with agony and bloody sweat, and water with plenteous blood and tears; yet, we must bring it to perfection, and pluck and eat thereof, or die. If we do not garner up that noble harvest for our children, better for those children that they had never been born.

There is no "Whole American people" — there are two — at least. And they are all opposed to "this war," but in two opposite senses. The New-Yorkers are opposed to our war, of defence —we are opposed to their war, of aggression. They and their rulers can stop when they choose, we and our rulers neither can nor will.

It is not strange that these people, coming of English race and trained in those English ways of freedom which our forefathers transplanted to this country, should have fought so bravely and so well; but it is strange, or if we did not know the influence of Slavery and an unsound cause, it would be strange, that as late as 1863, when they should have seen that the men of the Free States were at least as determined as they were, and twice as numerous and four times as rich, and were bent upon maintaining the Government, they would go on with this ever beginning, never ending brag.

(From the Richmond *Sentinel* of Sept. 4th, 1863.)

The North has a struggle to go through before she can prosper and be free — a struggle not with us, but with the elements of faction and crime in their own bosom. The cancer is there, and it must be cut out — the sooner the better. A war with the South does not mend the matter. It is not true that to stop the war with us is ruin to the North. We know not how a sane man can thus argue. To attain the firm ground of a prosperous society and a conservative Government, the course of the North is a plain one. The war with the South must be stopped, and that as speedily as possible. But this is only half the work. It is all that our interests absolutely require, but not all that humanity would teach other countries to do in their behalf. The conservative men of the North must put down and crush out the Abolition, infidel and agrarian element in their midst, before they can ever hope for solid peace in their own borders. Short of this, there is for them no safety; no hope of order, progress, or rational liberty. Let them dally with or postpone this duty, and severe convulsions, far eclipsing the French revolution, are before them. To accomplish this needful work, a revolution by arms is the necessary and proper means. Let them set to work at once. Lincoln may be apparently strong, but so was Robespierre before the Convention plucked up courage to oppose him. One bold effort by the Northern Democracy, and his power will topple to the ground, far more swiftly even than the edifice of tyranny was constructed. Nor will it cost much blood to effect it. It will most certainly not cost as much as will flow of their own blood from submission to a single conscription. And, when they get the power in their hands, they will do well *to show no foolish pity to any of the leaders of this Republican party* — to Lincoln, Seward, Greeley and the rest.

One and all they richly deserve the gallows; and if the Democrats fail to inflict the doom, in any case, upon these miscreants, the world will wonder, and history record it as a lamentable act of folly. This done, next let them proceed to establish a stable Government.

We all remember the advice, the adjuration, the denunciation which we received from the British press upon the subject of punishing Ex-Senator Davis; but although the above extract is a fair sample of hundreds of articles published upon its subject in the Slave State papers, who remembers one single article from the British journals denouncing this cry for the capital punishment of the Anti-slavery leaders.

"HARK FROM THE TOOMBS A MOURNFUL SOUND."

We find the following letter from Gen. Robert Toombs in the last number of the Sumter *Republican*:

Washington, Ga., Aug. 7, 1863.

MY DEAR SIR: Your letter of the 15th inst., asking my authority to contradict the report that " I am in favor of reconstruction," was received this evening. I can conceive of no extremity to which my country could be reduced in which I would for a single moment entertain any proposition for any union with the North on any terms whatever. When all else is lost, I prefer to unite with the thousands of our countrymen who have found honorable deaths, if not graves, on the battle-field. Use this letter as you please.

Very truly your friend, &c.,

R. TOOMBS.

Dr. A BEES, Americus, Ga.

At the present moment, in the language of his neighbors, Whar is Robert Toombs? Are he with the thousands of his countrymen who have found honorable death upon the battle field? No, my brethren, he are not. He are a layin off on a piazzy with his feet onto the railin, a chewing of the quid of rumination, and a laying of his plans to re-establish the Democratic Party and circumvent the Yankee Abolitionists in Congress.

THE CALL FOR THREE HUNDRED THOUSAND MEN.

Lincoln has made various proclamations since the commencement of the war, some of which have seemed to the world scarcely less unreasonable than those of the Chinese Emperor.

* * * * * * *

There must be an attempt at the facetious in the appeal for volunteers in default of which the draft will be made to work again. He knows well that no volunteers are to be expected in the future. In fact, it may be doubted whether the Yankee nation, between the disgust of those in the army and the servility of those out of it, are not reduced to the condition of the volunteer in the Mexican war, who so bitterly regretted his rashness that he swore never to do a voluntary act again. The volunteers will not be forthcoming and recourse must be had to the draft.

Were this extract to be closed here it would be impossible to tell from its style or its purpose whether it was published in the London *Times* or the Richmond *Examiner*. But the following paragraph, by its coarseness as well as by its boastfulness, shows its " chivalric " origin. It is from the Richmond *Examiner* of Oct. 27, 1863.

It is the debased inclination of a people who so lately arrogated the first place among the nations of the earth, and claimed the exclusive possession of the honor won for a common Government by the Southern people, who have forced a Roman's iron sceptre into the hands of a brute and a fool.

THE ATLANTIC TELEGRAPH
From the Richmond *Enquirer*, Nov. 3.

The Atlantic cable is certainly to be tried again. It appears that the indefatigable Mr. Cyrus Field has just come over from England to New York, bringing a specimen of the new cable manufactured by Messrs. Glass, Elliott & Co., and Yankees are largely taking stock. In other words, that stupid and blinded people is actually subscribing money to forge a chain for its own limbs. As before, the location selected for the cable places both ends of it on British ground, and therefore absolutely under British control. It signifies little what may be the constitution and by-laws of the company, as to keeping it entirely " neutral," and equally accessible to the two nations. All that kind of arrangement is good only for peace times; let war break out between England and the Yankees, and the Atlantic cable will be about as neutral as the Royal Artillery, and the Channel Fleet and the Horse Guards.

That British statesmen are looking forward to the recovery of the American colonies, and preparing to avail themselves of the exhaustion and anarchy which must succeed the present war, to attain that cherished purpose, is simply a matter of fact.

It is comfortable to be forewarned — not forearmed, that under the circumstances it would have been presuming to suppose — but to know our fate and be prepared for it before hand.

(From the Richmond *Enquirer* Nov. 3.)

If nothing were concerned in all this but the fate of the said Yankee nation, we should care but little. We might even look on with complacency while our stupid and troublesome neighbors at the North were weaving for themselves the web of their own fate. For ourselves, we hoped to be secured by the nature of our institutions against that acute malady of the American Republics which makes them rot at the heart, and fall before they are ripe. We hope, with God's blessing, to hold fast our liberties and our laws —to pay our debts and preserve order within our borders, so as not to afford to Kings and Queens those excuses and opportunities which the Palmerstons and Napoleons count upon so confidently. Yet it cannot be without some degree of concern that we shall see the British power reëstablish itself on the north bank of the Potomac. Who are to be our next door nebighors, is matter of some moment to us, and we confess that we should prefer the Yankees to the English in that situation: they would be a less danger to us, simply because they are less strong and less wise. Give us ignorant and semi-barbarous enemies to deal with, if we must have enemies; and on the north bank of the Potomac, for ages to come, we can look for nothing else but enemies. Therefore strongly incline to hope that this time again the Atlantic Cable will break and fall. Better for us that the Yankee nation should run its whole course of its raging fever, and end in the natural way than that England should come in, as Louis Napoleon is doing for Mexico, to "establish a permanent and responsible Government, under European guarantees."

In the meantime it ought to be agreeable to us to reflect that between us and Newfoundland lies the whole mass of the Yankee nation.

The English of which is, that about this time, November 1863, it was plain that all hope of intervention in any open, effective way, must be abandoned.

MORE BRITISH CANDOR AND GOOD FEELING.

(From the London *Times* of Feb. 1st., 1864.)

When Mr. M. Gibson gives his unreserved and unqualified homage to the Federal cause, he knows not of how much of a sort is his wisdom and that of the "model Republic," as it used to be called the other day.

As to the feelings of this country, it is true, we are not justified in regarding with exultation or satisfaction so terrible a calamity as that which has befallen so many millions of our own race. Nobody of common feeling does hear of the mutual slaughter and other sufferings entailed by the war, without commiseration. But while the Republic was overtopping and overshadowing us, while it stretched its limbs and raised its tones to the scale of a giant, it was impossible but that our sympathy should be weakened. We feel for men; not for giants, for monsters, for madmen, for those altogether out of our rank and species. But grant that the commercial injury is great, and that the general derangement of trade threatens to inflict even more serious injuries, yet it is impossible to prevent political considerations from intruding themselves, and even making a set-off the other way. Mr. M. Gibson cannot, surely demand from us that we should absolutely wish the United States to retain their "integrity," or now recover it, so as to make a vast political unity of the kind Mr. Bright describes? That would be to wish our own abasement and our own destruction.

Poor John Bull! You are then abased and destroyed, according to your own confession. But we don't see it. No one wishes to do you any harm; certainly not Brother Jonathan. And if you will only behave yourself and keep a civil tongue in your head, John, you will find yourself just as strong and just as prosperous as ever, and a good deal more respected.

THE SAME STORY OVER AGAIN.

(From the *London Times*, of Nov. 7, 1864.

Mr. Bright, of course, is not content with declaring his wish to see the United States once more as they were, and on the road to which the other day they hoped to be. Such a wish, under actual circumstances, we can hardly reconcile with belief in a man's soundness of mind. The best parallel that occurs to us is a wish to substitute the Heptarchy for a Monarchy now more than a thousand years old. Mr. Bright wishes more. He wishes to see the Union restored by the methods now in operation.

We take Mr. Bright upon his own showing. The wonderful image, overlaid with gold, and we know not how many cubits high, which he fell down and worshipped, has fallen to the ground and is broken to pieces. He wishes to see it once more on its legs, once more holding the globe on one hand, and a Victory, with outspread wings, on the other; once more with its foot on crowns and mitres, sceptres and chains. His disappointment is too much for him. He had faith in this. Here was a resting-place in the sea of change and the wreck of systems. Society stood here on its base, and not on its apex. The people here governed themselves without the cumbersome intervention of classes, and the fraudulent delegation of Emperors and dynasties. They were on the road to a millennium and human perfection, as social arrangements can bring it about. It was treason to think so grand a work of highest art could be "*fragile*," like the huge plaster images of a French spectacle. Yet such is the unhappy fact. It lies in fragments, which tell us how flimsy the material, how vast the internal cavities. No man ever yet saw without a pang of sympathy a child weeping over a broken pitcher, and we are heartily sorry for Mr. Bright. The largest and finest toy ever constructed by human ingenuity is a wreck, the glue melted, the sawdust run out, the wires broken, the colors departed. It is a most lamentable sight. At first we were as sorry as Mr. Bright could be; but we have long been convinced that it is no use to cry over spilt milk. The thing is done, and cannot be undone. But not such is Mr. Bright's philosophy. The image shall be pieced together, and shall be put on its legs, and men shall once more crawl in the dust before it.

THE LAWLESS DESPOTISM OF MR. LINCOLN.

(From the London Morning *Herald* of Nov. 5th, 1864.)

The convention of Chicago threatened loudly and boldly enough; and to judge by its confident phrases we might have thought that the Northern people were at last resolved to assert their rights with the courage worthy of freemen. But all menaces of armed resistance to unconstitutional violence have melted into smoke. Andrew Johnson of Tennessee, the Butler of the West, ordains that no citizen shall vote what does not take an oath to oppose the policy professed by General M'Clellan. [How true!] The general commanding at Baltimore suppresses, under threats of military violence, the organ of the Democratic party. Mr. Lincoln sustains the lawless outrages committed by his agents; and the opposition content themselves with angry murmurs. In several instances Mr. Lincoln has allowed or ordered the troops to fire upon Democratic meetings, and no resistance has been offered. [The Morning *Herald* strangely forgot to add that Mr. Lincoln ate the bodies of those persons at those Democratic meetings whom he allowed or ordered the troops to kill:— a fact the literal truth of which can be fully established.] It is plain then, that violence is to carry the day, and that for the first time in modern history the chief magistrate of a democratic republic is to be allowed to enforce his own re-election at the point of the bayonet.

Not by law, but in despite of law, Mr. Lincoln will continue President of the United States. His rule will be none the less effective because it will be utterly illegal; and his power will be none the less absolute that it rests not on popular suffrage, but on unconstitutional violence. The South has little reason to dread his success.

None whatever.

THE SAME SUBJECT CONCLUDED.

From the Morning *Herald* of Nov. 22, 1864.

In none of these States has election a meaning or an existence; **the** power is in the hands of military tyrants (who have **no more** authority to interfere with elections in America than in England, but who nevertheless surround every polling-place and enforce illegal oaths on every voter,) and the man who cast his vote for M'Clellan has done so at the risk of liberty, property, and even of life itself. He is an outlaw to whom the ruling authorities will give no protection; whose house may be burnt by Federal soldiers, whose cattle may be stolen by his Republican neighbors, whose letters will be opened in the post-office, whose family will be subject to menace and insult at the hands of Federal officers, and whose person may at any moment be carried off to undergo the discipline of labor with ball and chain in some military prison, or of solitary confinement in a fortress. No wrong done him will be punished; no right claimed by him will be granted. The military authorities would drive such a complainant from their doors ; the civil power has ceased, for all practical purposes, to exercise any functions whatsoever.

Were the simple facts of a case ever more plainly stated than in that paragraph? The British press is strong in its wisdom, strong in its good taste, but strongest in its truthfulness. And now let Munchausen hide his diminished head.

A BRITISH DESCRIPTION OF AN EMINENT AMERICAN.

(From the London *Morning Herald* of Nov. 23d. 1864)

We look, and perceive a community numbering millions in the North without a man of genius or of political probity wise or strong enough to counsel or to guide them aright. We see a military despotism never yet paralleled in Russia, in which the sceptre clinks the bayonet, and the bayonet sharpens the sceptre, both being weapons of spoliation and terror to society. Half a million of soldiers ravage one of the most generous regions of the globe. Future generations — if such are reserved for America — are daily shackled with hopeless debt. New England, the Far West, and the best old Puritan States, are bleeding to exhaustion. And Bishop Simpson's " missionary " is Abraham Lincoln, the mouther of stump speeches, the buffoon of the battle-field (after the battle is over) the concocter of humorous state documents upon questions of awful import to mankind, the swindler of the American constituencies, and the Judas of his country. A constitution violated, humanity outraged, Christianity scoffed at, war made fiendish — a thousand monuments of shame and ruin scattered over the land; and yet the maddened people seem proud of confiding that which Bishop Simpson proves their " destiny " to a desperado without one quality of demeanor or of intellect which would fit him to be more than a parish beadle. The only difference is that he can bluster, can corrupt, can select base instruments, can be mean and violent at the same time, can mock and jibe at misery, can ordain conscriptions, can play false with liberty, can scourge the press which made him what he has been, can gag the mouths of his fellow-citizens, and can be the hoot-owl of a direful conflict spreading its horrors from Canada to the Mexican Gulf, from the Atlantic to the Pacific Ocean.

The man meant was Abraham Lincoln

TWO OPINIONS

which appeared in the Richmond Correspondence of the London *Times*, December 5th, 1864.

GENERAL GRANT'S OPINION.

Information has just reached me of a conversation held last week, in which the interlocutors were General Grant and a gentleman who returned to Richmond on the 2d inst. from the North, bearing a letter of introduction to be presented *en route* from Mr. Seward to General Grant. It is well known that the gentleman in question (who is a foreigner) is in intimate relations with the Confederate Government. He paints General Grant as a gentleman of eminent courtesy, tranquil and dignified in manner, free from the proverbial bluster of his countrymen, and studiously conciliating in language. [Whoever heard of any one but a Yankee blustering? We all know that a Briton never blusters, and especially that he's always eminently courteous and studiously conciliating in language; of which this volume is filled with evidence.] He pointed out with emphasis that slowly and insidiously the Federal army is constantly advancing a step, and that never since the 14th of June, when it crossed to the South side of the James, has it made a quarter of a step backwards. "The end" he continued, "must be the fall of Richmond. How long it will be before the end comes it is impossible for me to say. General Lee knows the position of my army to be impregnable on both sides of the river, and he will attack on neither. I do not expect the city to be suddenly evacuated, but some day little by little my guns will get within shelling distance of the capital, and from that hour it is merely a question of time. It is probable that if at this stage the resistance be obstinate and prolonged, the whole city will be burnt to the ground. Anyhow its evacuation by General Lee's army is in the end inevitable."

THE TIMES CORRESPONDENT'S OPINION.

If General Grant could be induced to withdraw his eyes for a moment from the future of the Confederate States, and to contemplate the future of his own country, I would ask him to reflect in what estimation he is himself likely to be held by the fickle, many-headed beast of the North if he fails to take Richmond in the next six months? Many are the bitter Yankee-haters in this town, who wish for their enemies no greater degradation than that, having failed to subdue the South, they should find themselves with such a satrap as Abraham Lincoln strapped on their back for four years to come without hope of relief. Many are the vaticinations already heard in Richmond that the second *bustrum* of Mr. Lincoln, commenced in sunshine and tranquillity, and welcomed by a slavish and sycophantic community, will go out in storm and whirlwind amid execrations and curses. There is in the Arabian Nights no tale so wild and startling as a comparison between the wealth, progress, actual and prospective prosperity of the United States in 1860, and the utter humiliation of the record which they will exhibit in 1865.

THE CAPTURE AND SINKING OF THE FLORIDA.

The unjustifiable seizure of the rebel cruiser "Florida" was condemned at once by every journal of any position tion in the United States; it cost Captain Collins his ship and an open reprimand before the world. The sinking of the vessel in the night by a transport was equally deplored, and satisfactory apology and reparation was made to Brazil, one of the weakest powers in the world; yet the London *Times* which thus speaks of the affair in a leading article published December 31. 1864.

Having been sent to American waters, the Florida sunk in charge of a prize crew under circumstances which could excite the complacent approval of but one community in the civilized world. The whole transaction, including an ill-conditioned despatch from the Federal Minister in Brazil, must have afforded unqualified satisfaction to every enemy of the United States. The loss of honor is a very heavy price to pay for the destruction of a troublesome cruiser.

The "accident" will impose upon no one. Whether it will tend to exalt the character of the American people or that of their Government in the estimation of the world is a matter in which the majority of the Americans will give themselves no concern. It is a "smart Yankee trick;" and in a country where "smartness" ranks among the virtues the captain of the clumsy but effective transport which did the grateful mischief will doubtless expect to share the applause which has already been bestowed upon Captain

Collins of the Waschusett, and to be entertained at a public dinner by the solid men of New York. There is but small likelihood that he will be disappointed.

A marked instance this of the courtesy, the candor, and of the respectful consideration which is characteristic of every variety of the Anglo Saxon — except the Yankee!

THE WAR, PRESIDENT LINCOLN AND THE NORTHERN PEOPLE.

(From the Morning *Herald* of March 4, 1865.)

This is the Fourth Day of March, in the year 1865. It is a great anniversary for America. It is pencil-marked in the Book of her Constitution. Forty-eight hours hence a Senator will move, at Washington, that the United States, in gratitude for their prosperity and reputation do constitutionally acknowledge the existence of a Supreme Being. Whom, however, do they obey this morning? Once more Abraham Lincoln, who dispenses with all thought of a conscience or a future, trafficking in blood upon butcherly battle-fields, and crowning himself King of the New World Golgotha. The fourth day of March is doubly significant in the American annals. It brings the hour of the President's triumph; it was the day when, nearly two centuries ago, multitudes of red Indians assembled near the site of the present city of Philadelphia, moving through the woods in vast and dusky masses to ratify a treaty with William Penn. There, without banner, or mace, or guard, or chariot, the Quaker conciliated the Sachems; and well might the Sachems marvel could they witness the horrors which blacken around the heads of their successors in the American land. Their own barbarism is eclipsed; the civilization which was to supplant it is already extinct; the people talk vainly of God, and destroy his works without reason, compunction, or remorse. They propose to recognise a Supreme Being! And they deluge the soil with blood. Never was Chaos more profound. It is a huge wandering tumult from the shores of one ocean to the brink of another. It is a savage and shocking degeneracy of the human race. The world has witnessed spectacles equally startling; but where? No where, except in China, Hindostan, Egypt, and Tartary. Yet this is a people which offers to legalise a belief in the Deity!

And after years of such talk as this, the *Morning Herald* is one of the London journals that wonders why there is so much bitterness of feeling in the United States against Great Britain.

SUPPOSED CONSEQUENCES OF THE ASSASSINATION OF MR. LINCOLN.

(From the *London Times*, May 3, 1865.)

This terrible assassination has now occurred to snap and rend asunder all the speculations by which the chances of the future might be connected according to the lights before us, with the events of the past: and yet it is not certain that the prospect is changed for the worse. It is actually calculated, and perhaps with some reason that common grief and common indignation, just as they may draw Great Britain and America more closely together, may do the same for North and South. Nobody can tell how to forecast the possible results of the thunderclap. Of all the surprises of the revolution this is the most overwhelming. Never was a crisis so unfathomable in its import, or so completely beyond the scope of political divination.

And yet in spite of the thunderclap and the unfathomable crisis, events went on the day, the week, the month, for three months, after the assassination, just as regularly and as safely as they had done before.

CONCLUSION.

The foregoing pages leave no doubt as to the opinions and the feeling of the great majority of that part of the British people which is sufficiently intelligent and influential to make its voice heard in public, in regard to the great struggle which lately convulsed our country. But we are not left to inference upon this subject. We have positive testimony from British sources; of which the following paragraph from an article published in the Liverpool *Post*, in the beginning of the war, August 28th, 1861, is an example.

> We have no doubt whatever that the vast majority of the people of this country, certainly of the people of Liverpool, are in favor of the cause espoused by the Secessionists. The defeat of the Federalists gives unmixed pleasure, the success of the Confederates is ardently hoped, nay, confidently predicted.

The influence of this feeling upon opinion and in the direction of the moral force of the British people, was set forth by Mr. Taylor, (who is set down as a "Conservative,") in the House of Commons in July 1862. He spoke against a motion in favor of mediation, and in the course of his speech is reported as saying: —

> He regretted that the honorable gentleman had not accepted the advice to withdraw a motion which was without any possible advantage, and without any possible object except adding to the irritation and bitterness felt with regard to our position upon the question. The honorable gentleman said that, from reading the papers, he was inclined to think those feelings could not be worse. But he differed from him; and, although he admitted that exaggerated and mistaken opinions prevailed in the North, there was a great deal of ground for their bitterness and irritation. [Loud and repeated cries of "No."] America had a right to expect that, with our Anti-Slavery opinions, we should have looked with calmer eyes upon the struggle between the North and South. A certain portion, and a not uninfluential portion, of the English

Press has dealt anything but fairly with the Northern States. He hardly knew whether upon the merits or demerits of the Northern Government this portion of the Press was the most bitter. The censure was diverse and inconsistent. First, it was said to be ridiculous for a republic to attempt to go to war, and that it could not have that individuality of power necessary to enable it to strike a blow with effect; but when the Northern States showed that they would put down faction, and even give up individual liberty and the liberty of the Press, [hear!] they were called tyrannical and dictatorial. One day they were told that they could not carry on the war because they could not raise the money, and the next they were told that they were extravagant and thriftless in their expenditure. [Hear, hear!] They were denounced because they did not pass tax bills to raise revenue, and when the tax bills were passed, and the tariff increased, they were blamed for their bad policy. [Hear, hear!] They were denounced as hypocritical for professing to fight for the slaves, and yet as soon as they had shown distinctly the direction of their wishes by prohibiting Slavery in the central State of Columbia, they were told that they were not dealing justly with the State rights of the South. The amendment they were now discussing had been once or twice changed, and each time it was more diluted than before; but, no doubt, the honorable gentleman meant, by meditation, recognition of the South — [hear, hear!] — and intervention in the North. ["No! no!"] Intervention was only a longer word for war. Never was so tremendous an issue so easily, so lightly, and with so slight a recognition of its importance, raised. as had been this issue by the honorable member. [Hear.] It would be a fratricidal war, almost as truly as that which was being fought between the South and North — a war which would strike terror into all the friends of progress and liberty, and be rejoiced at by all who were their foes."

This is a testimony of a British Conservative. The following letter from a British Liberal, points out the same obliquity of judgment and unfairness of treatment in regard to this country and the war.

FEDERAL CRUELTIES.

To the Editor of the *Daily News*.

Sir: The *Times*, in a tirade against the Federals, says: "This war has been carried on with a cruelty which far surpasses anything which can be laid to the charge of England, though the lapse of 80 years has softened men's manners and has caused humanity to be respected even in the camp."

In our last war with America, only fifty years ago, Sir Charles

Napier witnessed the sack of Little Hampton by the British, and he states that on that occasion "every horror was perpetrated with impunity — rape, murder, pillage, and not a man was punished."

Further on, in his diary of the same war, he says: "Strong is my dislike to what is perhaps a necessary part of our job — viz. plundering and ruining the peasantry. We drive all their cattle, and of course ruin them. My hands are clean, but it is hateful to see the poor Yankees robbed, and to be the robber."

The *Times* talks, with the looseness of vague vituperation, about "towns burnt in diabolical wantonness." The burning of all the public buildings of Washington by the British is excused by British historians on the ground that the war between us and the Americans was "almost a civil war." There is only too much force in the excuse.

The standard of the British soldier's conduct, we may proudly say is on the whole as high in point of humanity as it is in point of valor. And judged by that standard, or by any other standard of military conduct known to history, the war on the Federal side has hitherto been remarkably humane. Not a single case of cruelty to a prisoner or a non-resistant, so far as I am aware, has yet been authenticated. Horrible stories were told of wholesale massacres and rape, but they have proved to be utterly unfounded. Gen. Butler's "massacres" at New Orleans' shrank into the military execution of a single Confederate for an outrage to the Federal flag which no commander could have overlooked, while two soldiers, as your correspondent informs us, were executed for maltreatment of the inhabitants. The wife of Gen. Beauregard lived in perfect security under the government of the Federal commanders. The violation of all the ladies in a boarding-school by Mitchell's men, with the sanction of their commander, seems to be completely disproved; at all events not an particle of evidence has been adduced in support of the charge. There has been great and cruel destruction of property by the Federals on land, and by the Confederates at sea; and the only difference between the two cases is, that the Confederate Government had partly effaced by its general impressments, the private character of property within its jurisdiction, while the private character of the property destroyed by the *Alabama* and her consorts remained uneffaced. The ravages of the *Alabama* were applauded by the House of Commons, and our Southern press was loud in its exultation over the great booty swept away from the Federal territory by the invading army of Gen. Lee.

The *Times*, the other day, published in large type, and in the most conspicuous part of the paper the letter of Capt. Semmes charging the commander of the *Kearsarge* with inhumanity in having willfully delayed to send boats to the assistance of the drowning men of the *Alabama*. In the same paper, but in small type and at the very bottom of the last column, appeared the intelligence that sixty-two of the *Alabama's* men saved *by* the *Kearsarge* had been landed at Cherbourg. The Captain of the *Kearsarge*, in spite of very exasperating circumstances, has treated his prisoners with chivalrous kindness, as the men themselves acknowledge. This we see, and we may judge from it of that which we do not see.

The massacre of the garrison of Fort Pillow by the Confederates, after surrender, is, on the other hand, perfectly authenticated. It is avowed by the Confederates themselves. The Southern journals in this country have found themselves compelled, in the interest of morality and justice, to pass it over in silence. The *Times*, however, had an allusion to it in a leading article, so worded as to lead its readers to believe that the atrocity had been committed on the Federal side.

The question whether free political institutions and free Christianity produce humanity, or the reverse, is one far transcending in importance the party question of this war, and hitherto, I venture to think, the result of the trial has been satisfactory to friends of freedom. I am, &c.,

GOLDWIN SMITH.

In fact, to use the words of a writer in the New York *Evening Post*, all the articles of the *Times*, and it might be added, of the *Saturday Review*, come to one practical conclusion; the utter incapacity, brutality and folly of the Americans of the North. It was lost in admiration of the skill of the four European nations which took just two years to capture the single fortress of Sebastopol; it had no terms in which to express its sense of the military energy that enabled Great Britain to put down the revolt of the Sepoys in about twenty-eight months; and it even lauds the success of the French in impoverished and distracted Mexico, who in the incredibly short time of twenty-three months have marched from Vera Cruz to the capital, a distance of one hundred and eighty-five miles, taking one fortified town on the way. But for the degenerate Yankees, who have been actually two years and a half in blockading five thousand miles of sea-coast, defending two thousand miles of menaced frontier, opening a river a thousand miles long in hostile possession on both banks, re-conquering two hundred and fifty thousand square miles of territory, and fighting hundreds of battles, some of them rivalling Waterloo in the numbers engaged — it has nothing but contempt. Such mournful proofs of imbecility in the government, of incapacity in the generals, of cowardice and lack of enthusiasm in the troops, and of complete moral indifference and corruption among the people, provoke its perpetual ire, and the choicest language of indignant vituperation.

Now for all this there was of course a reason. Such perversity is never spontaneous in a whole community of intelligent people; and the London *Times* one day naïvely confessed the how, the why, and the wherefore of all this misrepresention and abuse. It was done it seems from fear and with a motive; fear of republicanism, and in the hope of disgusting the British people with "the Great Republic." The *Times* admitted that we "could not be expected to view dismemberment of the Union without an effort to avert the loss;" and also that we had not shown any "peculiar incapacity for self-government." The following extract will show the gist of the leading article in question.

> We consider that the course of events in the Union has been perfectly natural, and that Americans have only done what Englishmen or any other people under the same conditions would have done also. What has so quickened our feelings and made our observations so acute is not so much the policy of America in itself, as the prominence which has lately been given to that policy by a certain party in this country. For the last ten years we have been told, with every circumstance of emphasis and adjuration, that American institutions were the institutions on which every friend of economy, peace and good government should fix his eyes. War was distinctly represented as the work of an interested aristocracy, anxious only for its own advancement. We were assured that with an unrestricted suffrage, and with electoral laws under which plain working citizens could make their voices heard, the old extravagance of a class government would rapidly disappear. Debts were contracted and wars were fought to gratify an aristocracy subsisting on the taxation of the people. America was the model of a better system. There the wisdom and moderation of citizens managing their own affairs showed itself in thrift and contentment. Such were the points kept obtrusively before us. If the reader will refer to any speech of any Manchester orator he will find the Government of the United States extravagantly eulogized for the very qualities of which it is now proved to be

utterly destitute, and the Americans exalted beyond all other people on account of gifts which it is plain that they never possessed. It is this, if the Americans wish to know the truth, which points the remarks of Englishmen on their civil war and its incidents. It is not that they are any worse, or more foolish or more intemperate than was to be expected under the trials to which they have been exposed, but that they have been held up to our admiration by a certain party among us as a people in whose counsels no intemperance or folly would ever be likely to prevail. They suffer from the panegyrics of their friends. Our extreme Liberals would have shaped the course of all British legislation exclusively by the American pattern; and, owing, indeed, to the position of parties, they did actually succeed in imparting now and then a transatlantic smack to the policy of the Government. When we look, therefore, at the operation of American institutions, we are contemplating the results of principles which it was sought to force upon ourselves. Such a lesson we cannot afford to lose. Our criticisms are suggested, not by any joy over American troubles, but by feelings of the deepest and most immediate self-interest.

In other words, the people for whom the *Times* spoke found it convenient and thought it proper to hound on the slave-holders' rebellion, and to hoot and howl at the government of the people of the Free States, in order to head off a political party at home. Well, they kept up a good cry, and we trust they are satisfied with the game they caught.

Another reason for this course of action and state of feeling, is given in the following extract from the Liverpool *Post* of August 28th 1864; which also sets forth truly how we were unjustly made to suffer for the faults of the very men whose cause the British press espoused.

The Americans have been boastful, offensive, and aggressive. Falsely assuming to themselves a power which circumstances have shown they did not possess, they have been defiant of the mother country, claiming a superiority to which they had not the remotest title. All this is true, and all this was bad: but it is too readily taken for granted that the Northerners did this and not the Southerners. Now, it so happens that the Southerners have been most to blame in the article of exaggerated presumption. They were in power; they occupied the White House; they sent Ministers to every Court in Europe; they appointed generals and admirals;

they quarrelled with us about Oregon, about the Mosquito territory, about rivers running into the Gulf, and about the islands in the Gulf. They bearded us when opportunity served, and they bearded us when we were not exactly in a condition to resent their insolence. The North may or may not have approved, but the North had no power; it was impotent for good or evil, in a political sense, until after the accession to office of Mr. Lincoln. In the phraseology of the stable, it is always desirable to put the saddle on the right horse; and at this moment, if people would abstract themselves from a prejudice which, after all, has been unjustly excited against the North, they would be in a better position to appreciate the merits of the South.

But beside all these causes of misunderstanding, there was one not so discreditable to the good sense and the candor of our British ill-wishers. They made the great, but not unnatural mistake, of forecasting our future by what are called the teachings of history; failing entirely to apprehend the vital fact, that the conditions of our political existence and our circumstances place us entirely without the range of any recorded precedent. The following extract from an article in the *Saturday Review* exhibits this erroneous judgment, and the false ground on which it is based.

SOUTHERN INDEPENDENCE AND NORTHERN LIBERTY.

(From the Saturday *Review* of Oct. 1st, 1864.)

European observers have long wondered at the sanguine hopes and eager credulity of the Americans of the Northern States — wondered to see the teachings of common sense and the warnings of experience alike set at nought, and expectations confidently entertained of which results seem to unexcited spectators simply impossible. Our Transalantic cousins have appeared to believe that the course of human nature would run in new channels in the Western hemisphere; that amity and good-will might be enforced at the point of the bayonet, and a Union resting on the voluntary coöperation of a multitude of independent democracies reëstablished by the victory of some over the rest. They have apparently thought that such a conquest as the greatest military Empires have never ventured to attempt might be achieved by the least warlike of Republics, and that, such conquest accomplished, it would leave behind it none of that rankling animosity, that incurable bitterness of feeling, which has in all other cases resulted, not only from the subjugation, but even from the humiliation, of a proud and high-spirited people. And they have so firmly cherished these ideas themselves as to accuse of ill-will, injustice, and obstinate prejudice those to whom such hopes appeared altogether chimerical. They have resented as a wanton insult, a proof of unscrupulous malevolence, the tendency of Englishmen to judge the prospects of America by the past experience of Europe, to believe that what has been is likely again to be, and that the invarible course of political events is not likely to be, for the first time, reversed in the issue of the present struggle between North and South. The Americans and their critics have utterly failed to understand each other. We have set down as evidence of simple political insanity their confident expectation of results at variance alike with historical experience and with the tendencies of human nature. We have reckoned it mere madness to believe that the South, with its enormous area, its impassable forests, its determined population, could be thoroughly subdued by any invader, or that the subjugation of the South could be otherwise than fatal to the existence of a Union of which local self-government and popular sovereignty are the fundamental principles. The Americans have been so confident in the destiny of the Union that they have been incapable of understanding an honest and impartial disbelief in its renewal. They have been so confident in their own wisdom, power, and patriotism, that they have treated the idea of a permanent overthrow of their liberties by the encroachments of that temporary despotism which the war has created as the wild and empty dream of impotent malevolence. We, knowing history better than we know America, have perhaps been too reliant on the lessons of experience. They, comparatively ignorant of any history but their own, have been blind to dangers which, however old in the experience of mankind, are so new and unforeseen as to seem incredible to them.

We could have afforded at any time to let the assertion that we are comparatively ignorant of any history but our own, pass with a quiet smile at the ignorance and rashness of the man who made it; and as to blindness to dangers which are old in the experience of mankind, and which threatened the overthrow of our liberties, it may possibly be safe to say at this moment, that if we could not see what did not exist it was hardly our fault, and that the wonderful provision of other people has not been so serviceable in discovering for us the fate to which we were destined, that we should mourn much over our own single sight and simple mind.

And now that we have thus refreshed our memories of the Rebel brag and the British bluster that we heard sounding, not only in accord, but in very unison, from the beginning even to the end of the rebellion, what shall we say and how shall we feel in regard to them? Are not these outpourings infinitely amusing? Do they not move us to laughter rather than to wrath? There is no doubt that they were meant to be insulting and injurious; and had our government failed to maintain itself, or had our war brought upon us any one of the many moral, material, and political disasters which were predicted for us, these insults might have added a drop of rankling venom to the wounds from which we should have suffered. But our present position is such that these British and Rebel orators and journalists stand before the world in a light so ridiculous as to be fit objects of our pity. And a moment's calm consideration will convince us that all this denunciation and disparagement is not the fruit of mere wanton malignity. Malignity will carry individuals, and even small bodies of men very far; but it will not lead great communities and the leading minds in great communities so far as to make them reckless equally of their reputation for good sense and of their interest. The truth is that all this offensive and absurd talk had its origin in ignorance,— ignorance which begot both prejudice and fear. Not fear in the nature of personal cowardice, or dread of our power; for there are probably no people in the world who have more personal courage or national hardihood than the British people, or our own countrymen in the late Slave States. The fear in question was not fear of us, but dread of our influence, of our example, and of our policy. The governing classes in Great Britain particularly feared, as the London *Times* virtually confesses in an article quoted above, that the effect of the continual prosperity of this Republic would be to deprive them of some of their privileges, to wrest from them some of their power, and distribute it among their people. They feared, too, that if we continued to increase in wealth and strength we should use our gigantic power after a giant's fashion, rudely, recklessly, and would keep the world in turmoil. How unfounded this latter fear was, we all know. It was the result of sheer ignorance and prejudice. The apprehension of the influence which the spectacle of the working of republican institutions, as we manage them, might have upon the people of Europe was better founded. But now that we have had our laugh at this nonsense, and have seen that it really was the result of ignorance and vague apprehension, as appears by almost every line of it, shall we not be wiser and worthier of our position and our strength, if instead of laying it up against our baffled ill-wishers, we pass it by as the natural consequence of their incompetence to grasp the situation which we have mastered, and think of it, if we think of it at all, with serene indifference and good-nature?

THE END.

www.ingramcontent.com/pod-product-compliance
Lightning Source LLC
Chambersburg PA
CBHW020145170426
43199CB00010B/894